SECRETLY
AND
OFTEN

*The Journey
of Prayer*

VICTOR THOMAS

WESTBOW
PRESS®
A DIVISION OF THOMAS NELSON
& ZONDERVAN

WestBow Press books may be ordered through booksellers or by contacting:

WestBow Press
A Division of Thomas Nelson & Zondervan
1663 Liberty Drive
Bloomington, IN 47403
www.westbowpress.com
844-714-3454

Unless otherwise indicated, all Scripture quotations are from New Revised Standard Version Bible, copyright © 1989 National Council of the Churches of Christ in the United States of America. Used by permission. All rights reserved worldwide.

Scripture taken from the King James Version of the Bible.

ISBN: 978-1-6642-1400-2 (sc)
ISBN: 978-1-6642-1401-9 (hc)
ISBN: 978-1-6642-1399-9 (e)

Library of Congress Control Number: 2020923484

Print information available on the last page.

WestBow Press rev. date: 12/29/2020

To my mother and first prayer mentor, Rachel. To my
wife, Nicole; my daughters, Brianna and Brielle; and my
son, Bryce. To the parish of Saint James', Houston

contents

foreword

Both Jesus and Saint Paul taught we should always be praying "without ceasing," that is, living life with an attitude of prayer (Luke 18:1 and 1 Thessalonians 5:17).

Prayer is the most essential gift we have as Christians because it is the path to an intimate relationship with God. Without the practice of a prayerful living, how do we find our moral compass? How do we survive material and human loss? How do we know the joy of God's saving and refreshing presence in our lives? And most importantly, how do we have a life of conversation with God? How do we pray? Yet, the fact is, we live in very complicated times, times in which political interest, professional ambitions, and economic demands easily sublimate intimacy with God and spiritual health. So how do we reclaim this rich and beautiful gift of a prayer and intimacy with God?

In the Gospels, Jesus taught about the essential nature and gift of prayer in our lives. But more importantly, the Gospel record of his life and ministry is replete with examples of his prayer life, his intentional conversations with God. We read of Jesus "turning aside" or "going to a lonely place" for private prayer in the midst of a busy day, of spiritual retreats on a mountain or in a garden or olive grove with his disciples (or "friends," as he called them). We read, many times, he "lifted up his voice" and offered prayer in the midst of multitudes and, of course, in times of distress and personal doubt, such as on the cross.

Many Christians, in considering Jesus's prayer life, forget he considered regular participation in congregational worship essential. In Luke 4:16, we learn that Jesus "...went to the synagogue on the sabbath day, as was his custom." Jesus not only taught that Christians must live in a spirit of prayer, he knew it was essential in his own life and ministry. There is an African American spiritual that says, "If Jesus had to pray, what about me?"

But it is difficult to keep a focus on a prayerful life in such politically and morally complex times. Our distorted passions for material security and economic wealth also cause our lives to be a living prayers for material prosperity and security above all else. The Psalmist mirrored this reality and its consequence when cautioning his own generation: "And God gave them the requests; but sent leanness into their souls" [Psalm 106:16]. However, I am noticing that Christians and seekers of many stripes—evangelical, progressive, traditional, and nonaffiliated—are becoming aware of their "leanness of soul." Many are seeking a deeper relationship with God. Should you or someone you know hungers for an authentically deeper prayer life, this book is for you. I know reading it has been a gift to me, refreshing my spiritual journey.

I am particularly grateful this book is written by a seasoned parish pastor. A unique quality throughout this book is its pastoral nature and tone. Reading this book, one senses a caring pastor is with them as each chapter reveals the meaning, practice, and ways of the prayerful life. As it is with a faithful pastor, the author knows intimately the power of prayer in times of the soul's leanness because he has walked with us. The high privilege of a pastor is praying with others in times of celebration, failure, ill health, deep disappointments, occasions of confession, and in the "shadow of death." A pastor who prays with us on our life's journeys brings a unique, caring, and accessible wisdom to the teaching of prayer and the spiritual life. *Secretly and Often* has that unique quality.

While the author does draw upon the insights of theologians and mystics and the wisdom of his own spiritual mentors, what makes this text valuable is his clear insights into the fundamentals modes of prayer and his empathy regarding the challenges to a prayer life in everyday living. From this vantage, the author considers our prayers in the pew, particularly the resources of the *Book of Common Prayer*, and how our journeying in a chaotic and complex world can be lived in intimate conversation with God.

For those seeking a deeper richer understanding and practice of prayerful living, *Secretly and Often* will be a gift for a lifetime.

The Rt. Rev. Nathan D. Baxter, DMin, STD, DHL, DST, DD

Tenth Bishop of Central Pennsylvania (retired)

Former Dean, Washington National Cathedral

acknowledgments

For the 2018 Vestry of Saint James' and their Senior Warden, Joseph Jones, PhD, who encouraged me to complete this project and approved sabbatical time in order to make sure it happened.

For Loyce McAfee, who relentlessly pursued content approvals for me. For my staff, who are true co-laborers in the work of Jesus the Messiah.

introduction

Perhaps you think you don't know enough about prayer to feel you will be effective. If you want to pray but find it difficult to stay consistent, you are in good company. If you are aware of the great value in constant communication with God but the busyness of life, lack of motivation, and numerous things competing for your attention, your experience is similar to every great Christian that's gone before you.

Secretly and Often focuses more on *why* we pray rather than *how*. The endless reasons for prayer will always trump the methods. I believe exploring the reasons for ongoing communication with God will serve us well and become a source of future motivation. Most of us practice and succeed in an area when we are clear on why it's needed. Immediately in this book, we establish the *why* of prayer. Then in the successive chapters we continue to drill down on how the why extended itself through the various forms of prayer.

I wrote *Secretly and Often* in order to partner with you to rethink what it is to talk to the Creator and underscore how prayer is more than rattling off desperate petitions in times of crisis. I wrote this not as an expert and guide but as a fellow practitioner and cotraveler on this faith journey. You and I walk the same road to follow Jesus. Our trip together will take us through different forms of prayer—petition and supplication, praise, Thanksgiving, confession, and penitence.

That said, many of my references for the above forms of prayer come from the 1979 *Book of Common Prayer* of the Episcopal Church, which is the worship tradition that anchors me in the gospel of Jesus Christ. However, this is a book for the entire church because every tradition more or less practices the same types of prayers.

My hope is to whet the appetite of the reader around the deep need we have to talk with God. Of all the things that are happening within the universal church, intimacy with God will always be first and foremost. It has, and always will, serve as the ground for all of the other activity that takes place in the life of Christianity. No program can substitute for it. No council resolution can take its place. Prayer is the only road to intimacy with God.

one

WHY PRAYER?

"If there is anything you will learn from me, Father, it will be how to pray," he declared. As he sat opposite me, crossing his legs and wearing a white cassock with red buttons and rim, his eyes were filled with both kindness and intensity. He then uncrossed his legs and leaned forward, clasping his hands together and resting both elbows on his knees. "We will pray twice a day, morning prayer and evening prayer. All of us will be at our prie-dieu"—prayer desk—"at eight thirty in the morning, and we will return at five thirty in the evening to pray again. Wherever you are and whatever you are doing, you will stop and leave to give yourself enough time to get back to the church. This is not an option. Prayer will mark the rhythm of the work we do together. If you come here, this will be our life together."

I nodded my head as he spoke. Although I did so in an affirming fashion, communicating that I was completely on board, inside me some uncertainty welled up. I thought, *I'm all for prayer but what am I getting myself into?*

Why don't we pray more? Why aren't our prayers filled with more passion and drive? Why don't we have greater confidence that God will indeed answer our prayers? Why do we have so many false starts, half-hearted attempts, and interrupted prayers? We know prayer is important—really important—but for some reason, the ability to do it eludes us. It is so important that the scripture goes as far as to command us with these three words: "pray without ceasing, " (1 Thessalonians 5:17).

Those who begin to dedicate themselves to prayer will soon discover how much work it really is—arduous, involved work. There are times we would rather do anything but pray. We may find ourselves laboring with and through our communication with God, exhausted just by the thought of engaging in it when we see how much work is involved. As my professor of pastoral care in seminary, the Reverend Charles Wellington Taylor, once said, "Prayer is hard work, and there's a reason why the Episcopal *Book of Common Prayer* calls daily prayer 'The Prayer Office.'" Everyone knows what takes place in an office: work.

Does prayer only involve work? Of course not. But it wouldn't be honest to withhold how labor-intensive it is to maintain a prayer life. The good news is that apart from the work aspect of prayer, there is an intimacy with God created only through prayer. In Mark 14:36, when Jesus prayed and called God the Father, *Abba*, or "Daddy," he provided us with a preview or coming attraction of the intimacy we could have in prayer. Many found this notion mind-blowing in Jesus's time, because referring to God in such a familiar and loving manner was unheard of among the Jews. In an instance, Jesus demonstrated how weighty and dynamic a relationship with God can be. He demonstrated that we can have a relationship with God that is filled with confidence, allowing us to pour our hearts out to him.

Even during the more mundane times, we can still sense a palpable closeness to him. So beyond creeds, doctrines, and denominations, the clearest and most basic expression of our faith is prayer. The classic Latin expression *lex orandi; lex credendi* holds true: "The rule of praying is the rule of believing." For Christians everywhere, this is not only an expression of fact but a solemn admonition; if we believe, we will pray. Furthermore, if the faith we confess is central to our lives and God is everything we say He is to us, we will be people of prayer.

This intimacy-building characteristic of prayer is found only in the act itself. It is not derived from simply thinking about it, talking about it, or reading books about it, but through the daily practice of prayer and talking to God on behalf of oneself or others. I have been both amused and inspired by the stories of the great prayer giants of the past. Martin Luther, one of the fathers of the Reformation, would pray no less than three hours to be ready for his day. Charles Simeon was known to pray from the hours of four to eight every morning. Bishop Lancelot Andrewes engaged in at least five hours of prayer and devotion each day. For John Wesley, the father of Methodism, it was important to maintain a habit of prayer lasting at least two hours in duration.[1] Pope John Paul II modeled great dedication in this holy practice, spending up to six hours in prayer in one session.[2] Evidently, most great people of prayer spend much time communicating with God. They find prayer to be indispensable in their work for God. Prayer may not have been their heart's desire at the beginning, but it grew to be, becoming a necessity.

The late archbishop of Canterbury, Robert Runcie, known for his brilliance and tireless work ethic, once engaged in a conversation with his clergy in which he displayed complete command of theology, church history, and philosophy. Following the meeting, one of his assistants asked him, "Lord Runcie, I know your schedule and all the demands on you. How is it that you find the time to read enough to have such deep and broad knowledge on so many subjects?"

Runcie answered, "I approach my reading like an alcoholic approaches his drink—secretly and often," thus calling attention to the fact that we need to be just as energetic, resourceful, and persistent with virtuous activity as we are with our vices.

I believe this same principle of "secretly and often" was applied by those who have been powerhouses in prayer. Those repetitive, stolen moments of prayer served as the kindling for the spiritual infernos their lives would become. They possessed and maintained a spiritual disposition that drove them to pray at every opportunity during travel, between engagements, and during mundane meetings as well as in times of great need or tragedy. The result was intimacy, which is both inspirational and transformative.

---

[1] E. M. Bounds, E. M. Bounds on Prayer, Whitaker House, 1997, 486.
[2] Edward Pentin, "Pope John Paul II Scourged Self, Prayed for Hours," NewsMax, Nov. 24, 2009

❖ *Formation*

In the same way prayer functions as the currency of divine intimacy, it also serves as the apparatus for spiritual formation. If you step outside and direct your gaze at the night sky, you will soon notice two stars. Conspicuous because of their greater brightness, the stars Betelgeuse and Rigel serve as address markers for Orion's belt. Nearby is the Orion nebula, a stellar nursery for newborn stars. A nebula serves as the birthplace for stars on a galactic level, just as prayer serves as the birthplace of social justice, relevant theological questions, and true comfort. Anyone involved in Christian formation will tell you that it isn't so much about the dissemination of theological and biblical information as it is about helping people think theologically and ask rich and relevant questions.

For a long time, churches have focused on two things: worship and Christian education. In recent years, many denominations have replaced the term *Christian education* with *Christian formation*, which includes education and everything else the church has to offer. Information, outreach, worship, and education come together to form the entire person into a disciple of Jesus who can carry on to promote his presence in the world. It's not enough to know about God. Formation is focused on knowing God through an informed and intentional process. Prayer is instrumental to the formation process. Formation combines knowledge *about* God and intimacy *with* God. More than facts and data, formation leads us to experience an encounter that gives hope for even our deepest doubts and most crippling fears. In a sense, prayer becomes the software that runs our lives, proving that the hardware is still working. Thus, to be formed in the Christian faith is to take the stories and principles of the Old and New Testaments, the biographies of great saints, the history of the Church, and the theology of the faith, and knit them together through prayer like a quilt. Instead of old, disconnected ideas and experiences, this quilt becomes relevant and a living companion for our journey of faith.

> "The function of prayer is not to influence God, but rather to change the nature of the one who prays."
> —Søren Kierkegaard

Kierkegaard's statement should be the church's ongoing desire and vision for every child who enters a Sunday school class for the first time.

❖ *What Is Prayer?*

The catechism of the *Book of Common Prayer* defines prayer as communication with God. Other definitions serve us well when we consider what prayer really is. Yet even in our best attempts to define it, we will never be able to explain prayer fully. Communication with God is only the tip of what prayer can be. The greater part of it remains hidden from our understanding, just as the largest and most dangerous part of an iceberg is hidden from our sight.

The theologian Leonard Sweet gave a good example of what happens in prayer. The thoughts of the mind can be detected in wavelengths. We are given an opportunity to interact with the mind of God and be on the same wavelength as the divine when we pray. Of course, Isaiah 55:8 says, "'For my thoughts are not your thoughts, nor are your ways my ways,' says the Lord." because his thoughts are on a higher and more meaningful level than ours. However, when we enter in prayer, we tune ourselves to the wavelength of God. For the narcissist, this attunement could be an opportunity to pontificate and become delusional. But for the sane and earnest, it is a humbling idea. The latter produces an experience absent of any self-exaltation and instead creates genuine thankfulness for the opportunity to communicate with the Creator of the universe.

Prayer is not only communication but also a spiritual disposition, one in which we develop and maintain divine reliance, openness, and genuine self-reflection.

The role of honest questioning and even doubt are rarely mentioned yet vital in prayer. Those who are truly dedicated to prayer experience periods of real doubts, during which they find themselves facing questions that are difficult to answer. When we embrace questions with the arms of faith, our thoughts are transformed and our souls flourish. Resolution even emerges in some cases. Conversation with God contains tension and the actual risk of unanswered questions. When a family member is suffering or a marriage dies, questions surface. In 2003, I sat before my television, horrified by the image I had just witnessed. A little boy, perhaps four or five years old, was playing alone on the beach. Out of nowhere, an enormous wave engulfed the child and swept him away. With my mouth agape in shock, I witnessed a tsunami's destructive power. I was heartbroken. I'm not naïve; I have experienced as much as the next person and am aware of the many changes life can bring about. But as a father, the shock in that moment stayed with me. And it had me questioning.

I should not have been surprised by it because, theologically, I know the difference between moral and natural evil. Moral evil is committed by human beings through the volition of their wills. Hitler's Holocaust of the Jews is a textbook example of a moral evil act. Stalin's planned starvation and execution of entire communities meet the moral evil criteria. Pol Pot and the Khmer Rouge's violent purge of all artists, teachers, and community leaders from Cambodia has moral evil written all over it. Finally, the most recent incarnation of moral evil is the terrorist organization known as ISIS, who continue to take a page from the medieval playbook of barbarism and sectarian hatred. These are the epitome of moral evil. Natural evil, on the other hand, involves acts of nature. A tornado that spins through a town, destroying everything in its path and stealing human lives, is an example of natural evil. We can label famine, earthquake, yellow fever, polio, and the recent outbreak of Ebola as other examples of natural evil.

Then there are times when moral and natural evil combine forces to cause destruction. Out of nowhere, an earthquake can hit, causing a house to collapse and killing its inhabitants. The death toll could have been less or eliminated altogether, but the builder had used subpar materials during construction, and no one had the courage to question his decisions. On Monday, May 14, 2008, a 7.9-magnitude earthquake rattled China's southwestern province of Sichuan, causing the collapse of numerous schools and killing over a thousand students and teachers. There was no doubt about the natural evil's role in it as an earthquake, but it was later found that moral evil was at work as well, in the form of cost-saving but corrupt building practices. Buildings should have been designed to withstand such an earthquake but were instead designed to withstand far less. There was no reason to have had such a large loss of life. Witnessing evil, whether natural or moral, to any degree can drive a wedge between a person's desire to pray and their belief in the effectiveness of prayer.

Honest prayer embraces all this—the good and the evil, the apathy and the heartfelt commitment—and it turns it back to God. Real prayer says, "God, I remain in conversation with you about what pains and bewilders me. I will keep coming back to you with the questions I have about what I can't explain or understand." As my rector had mentioned in the beginning of the chapter, prayer is the process of faithfully coming to the prie-dieu (prayer desk) with regularity—not just when it is convenient. Thus, the difficulties and questions of life rub against our belief in a God who comforts and acts.

TYPES OF PRAYER

two

PRAYERS OF ADORATION
AND PRAISE

W hat exactly is adoration and praise? Most Christian denominations seems to have a written explanation of these two terms. Meanwhile, some churches may have no written description but are nonetheless experts of them in prayer. In my denomination, the Episcopal Church, we have a definition of adoration and praise in the catechism of the 1979 *Book of Common Prayer* (p. 587).

Q. What is adoration?
A. Adoration is the lifting up of the heart and mind to God, asking nothing but to enjoy God's presence.
Q. Why do we praise God?
A. We praise God, not to obtain anything, but because God's Being draws praise from us.

The prayer book's explanation of it is thorough, serving as a starting point to discover its deeper facets. Adoration and praise are forms of prayer in which we give glory to God. It's not in connection with anything we received, but rather, it is a meaningful response to the greatness of God's being.

For many, expressing prayers of adoration and praise is a challenge. For some, they don't have the language for it. For others, it seems silly to flatter God. Then there are others for whom adoration and praise are difficult to express because they personally never received praise. People who received little praise in their lives can find it difficult to give praise to anyone, even when a person's progress or accomplishments are obviously deserving of praise. Thus, although this inability can be deep-seated and complicated, it does not mean one cannot grow to regularly praise those around them who deserve it and to continually praise God, who always merits it.

Offering praise and adoration can be difficult specifically because of the way most of us tend to think today. Most of us think from a forensic perspective, perhaps due to the work we do. The word *forensic* comes from the Latin word *forensis*, which means "in open court." It's a way of thinking that involves judgment. To think this way means everything we come across is on trial. And it can be a difficult habit to shut off because you been judging all day; every situation you encounter, you find yourself judging it. In Jesus's day, the Pharisees and Sadducees picked apart and judged his every action, even those that were clearly helpful. They had, in a sense, arrested him and placed him on trial long before the garden of Gethsemane. Things haven't changed much in the last two thousand years. Every little thing around us falls under judgment or is on trial. It's hard to turn off once you leave the office. That's how you are at work, and when you take it home, your family will say, "Hold on, cowboy. This is not the office." They are right. It's not like you can write up your spouse or your kids. "That's it, I'm going to write you up." No, it doesn't work. For some of us, it is hard to praise other people, let alone God. But if you praise God, you will also find yourself with the ability to praise people too. They will not be on trial in your mind.

So when we practice adoration and praise, something different is at work. Our tendency to judge is removed, and we stand before the presence of God with a mindset to give praise.

The word *adoration* means "to worship." It also denotes the placing of something—or in this case, someone—on a pedestal. In this instance, instead of being forensic (judging and placing on trial), we opt to adore because adoration is the only proper response to what is before us.

❖ *Why Do It?*

Years ago, several books on adoration and praise were released, outlining its benefits and explaining how it empowers believers who put it into practice. As a result, some people misunderstood the authors of these books and used praise and adoration to get God to do something for them. Whether intentional or not, some people's praises teetered on the edge of divine manipulation. But God cannot be manipulated.

We praise and adore because we are called to praise God. The Bible points to this in Psalm 34:1, where it says, "I will bless the Lord at all times; his praise shall continually be in my mouth."

When we are in the presence of true greatness, we can't help but lavish praise.

In nearly half of Jesus's prayers, he erupts in spontaneous praise. In the garden of Gethsemane, Jesus lifted up prayers of adoration and praise when he prayed in John 12:28, "Father, glorify your Name." In Luke 10:21, Jesus sent out seventy-two of his disciples, commanding them to heal the sick and perform exorcisms. Upon their return and report of success, Jesus expressed spontaneous adoration and praise. Also, when Jesus raised Lazarus from the dead, ordering him to come out from the tomb after being dead for exactly four days, spontaneous adoration and praise poured forth from the lips of the Messiah. In short, if he did it, we should too.

All of God's creation declares His greatness. Renowned author and pastor of the Bethlehem Baptist Church in Minneapolis, John Piper believes in praise and adoration so much that he preaches once or twice a year on the greatness of God alone, with no application whatsoever. He would simply stand there and tell people how of God's greatness. Not once does he follow it up by saying, "This is how it applies to you." He is convinced of John 12:32 where Jesus said: "And I, when I am lifted up from the earth, I will draw all people to myself." By lifting Jesus up in this manner, by adoring him and praising him, Pastor Piper exposes his congregants to the power of adoration and praise.

This reminds us of how amazing God is and how He should be set above all. We see this reminder in everyday life. For example, as children, our parents likely warned us not to touch the fine china. Before we learned our ABCs, we knew better than to touch it. It was special, reserved for significant occasions, and it spent most of the time in a distinct cabinet. Among all the dinnerware in the house, our mothers valued it most and placed it on a pedestal. Granted, china pales in comparison to God, but if we are willing to go through so much trouble to adore a lesser and lower thing, how much more willing we should be to honor and adore the almighty God, the Creator of the universe.

Through praise and adoration, the Holy Spirit says to us, "Yes, you've got real problems, but God is bigger than your problems." In Numbers 13:1–33, Moses sent twelve spies to investigate the land of Canaan and its inhabitants. When they saw the people of Canaan, only two came back with a good report, and the other ten produced a negative report; yet they saw the same thing. Only two saw the challenges their nation faced through the lenses of faith, remembering the power of the God. I witnessed something like this in practice in 2016, in my wife's grandmother's life. One of her daughters, my wife's aunt, had died after a long and hard battle with cancer. Then, to add insult to injury, on the morning of the funeral, while the family was preparing to go to the church for the burial service, my wife's grandfather died. My wife's poor grandmother was overcome with grief, having her husband die on the same day they were to bury their daughter. Yet at both funeral services, her audible expressions of praise and thanksgiving were profound: "I praise you, Lord. Oh, I praise you, mighty God." Despite the pain and the great trial, she praised God.

Why praise and adore God? Because He is worthy of it. So many times, we think of prayer as coming to Him and asking for something. Admittedly, a request is part of prayer. But when we praise His presence, something profound happens. We are giving something back to him by offering him praise and adoration; we break free from the whirlpool of our own concerns and find dry ground in God's true glory. And we are not worried about what we look like, what we gave, what we are wearing, or who is seeing us.

❖ *So How Do We Practice Adoration and Praise?*

In a practical sense, we are to come to God first with praise and adoration. Like with anything else, you need to start small, which you will discover is applicable to prayers of petition and prayers of intercession. The same also applies with praise and adoration. Some need to start small because it's awkward to sit up and say, "God I praise You. God, I worship and adore You. God, You are great. There is no one like You, and You are worthy of all honor, glory, and praise."

Before you start doing anything else or begin asking for anything for yourself or others, start praising God first. That is your starting point.

To focus your mind on God's greatness, simply consider His glorious work of creation. If He is, indeed, the Creator of the universe, then ponder His sheer immensity. The best minds in physics, astrophysics, biology, genetics, and geology, to name a few, dedicate countless hours in understanding the glory of His creation. We find out new, amazing information on it regularly. Consider this: At one time, we thought the universe was confined to the limits of the Milky Way galaxy. When the Hubble telescope was invented, cosmologists found thousands of galaxies in a single cluster, which means the entirety of space contains several hundred billion galaxies. Furthermore, there are more stars in space than there are individual grains of sand on all the beaches of the earth. Is that not mindboggling? The universe and world we live in can forever produce a sense of wonder within us. Every year, we are finding out more and more about them.

Another way is to ponder the miracle of human life. Each one of us is a living, thinking human being, given the ability to create and improve what we make. We need not look far for miracles because each one of us is a walking miracle. Consider also the beauty of a sunset. As our sun slowly ducks beneath the horizon, the sky becomes the canvas for a spectacular piece of artwork painted by the hand of God. For centuries, artist and photographers have tried to capture its beauty, but nothing can come close to representing how gorgeous a sunset is to the naked eye.

So with these in mind, think about God's greatness and praise and congratulate him for it. In a sense, become his cheerleader. You will find a sense of appreciation, awe, and wonder begin to fill your mind. If the words "You are worthy of praise" seemed silly, they will no longer be, as they will flow from a place of deep reflection. The apostle Paul experienced this deep reflection when he wrote in Philippians 2:9–11, "Therefore God exalted him to the highest place and gave him the name that is above every name, that at the name of Jesus every knee should bow, in heaven and on earth and under the earth, and every tongue acknowledge that Jesus Christ is Lord, to the glory of God the Father."

If you continue to have a hard time saying words, read aloud Psalms 19, 33, 103, and 145 to 150 before your prayer. By doing so, you are still praising and adoring God until you find your own way of expressing it.

Things happen first by inspiration and imitation. After some time, our praise and adoration will originate from a place deep inside us. We will cease to copy others in praise and become our own fountains of praise.

Psalm 150 says:

> [1]Praise the Lord!
> Praise God in his sanctuary; praise
> him in his mighty firmament!
> [2] Praise him for his mighty deeds; praise him
> according to his surpassing greatness!
> [3] Praise him with trumpet sound;
> praise him with lute and harp!
> [4] Praise him with tambourine and dance;
> praise him with strings and pipe!
> [5] Praise him with clanging cymbals; praise
> him with loud clashing cymbals!
> [6] Let everything that breathes praise the Lord!

Praise the Lord!

1. E. M. Bounds, *E. M. Bounds on Prayer*, Whitaker House, 1997, 486.
2. Edward Pentin, "Pope John Paul II Scourged Self, Prayed for Hours," NewsMax, Nov. 24, 2009.

three

PETITION: WHEN WE ASK GOD, GOD ANSWERS

It's important that I pray on it before I mess it up.
—Ben Okoh, Lay Preacher in the
Episcopal Diocese of Texas

❖ *What Is the Prayer of Petition?*

To petition is to make a request already known to God. It's asking God to do something on our behalf. It is also referred to as supplication. A petition is the basic experience in prayer because it requires our energy to make a request of God out of our need. Pleading with a power greater than oneself to meet a real need is a common human experience. Have you ever needed anything? Have you ever needed something to happen for you? If you have—and all of us have—you might've approached God in a prayer known as petition.

Petition is more than simply asking God for something. It is the expression of a trusting heart calling out to God who is trustworthy, cloaked in the language of dependence. This demonstrates our human limitations and our reliance on God's unlimited ability.

Think of it: Two thousand years ago, Jesus's disciples and friends looked him in the eye and requested, "Teach us how to pray." In response, he gave them what we now call the Lord's Prayer. Most of the prayer consists of petition. Asking God "to give us this day our daily bread" is considered a petition. We are asking God to care for our needs. Sometimes, the petition is a request to help us care for our needs as they relate to our worship of Him. God may at times do so in ways we could not do on our own. President Woodrow Wilson once said, "In the Lord's Prayer, the first petition is for daily bread. No one can worship God or love his neighbor on an empty stomach."

No matter how the daily bread comes, there's always a petition asking God to be involved in getting it; He can help us so our needs would not overwhelm us. I love the petition in Proverbs 30:8–9:

> [8] Remove far from me falsehood and lying; give me neither poverty nor riches; feed me with the food that I need, [9] or I shall be full, and deny you, and say, "Who is the Lord?" or I shall be poor, and steal, and profane the name of my God. The goal of petition is to ask God to do something for us, with a desire to honor Him.

❖ Weighing the Intent of Our Petitions

There have been some issues around prayers of petition. Some have been so caught up in petition that they pray about everything. They are the type to make requests for parking spaces and who ask God to make sure that their favorite type of sandwich is available in the cafeteria. It is one thing if you're running late for an important appointment, you enter a packed parking garage, and everything is on the line if you're late. The need to pray for a parking space is then understandable. But it's a different issue to make the same request just because you want a good space for your shopping spree. It is likely due to the belief that everything we ask for should be granted to us. Whenever this attitude of entitlement exists, there can be excess.

However, there is the other side of the coin—those who don't believe in petition at all. They don't mind praying for other people, which is intercession. Neither do they mind liturgical forms of prayer, but they have a problem with going to God personally with a request for themselves and their needs. It may be that they believe God has other, more important things to do, so they do not want to bother him with something they believe they can handle themselves—no matter how big the issue might be.

Or it might just be due to pride. We might come before God regularly and pray for other people but believe that we need not to pray for ourselves. When considering this, it is important to remember the words of King James version of Proverbs 16:18: "Pride cometh before the fall." We forget that we need to petition God to have the spiritual strength we need to weather the storms of life. Petition is a vital and important ministry work that we are entrusted to do. Both frivolity and complete neglect in petition must be avoided.

As a Christian, the more open I am with God about my journey, the deeper my relationship with Him becomes, and the less inclined I am to be frivolous in asking. Petition becomes a relationship of exchange, a true back-and-forth, when I have conversations with the Almighty. When petition becomes part of a thoughtful process, I am more inclined to be humble when I am tempted to handle all my problems on my own. It's as though I enter a mindset wherein I recognize my true dependence on God. When I am in such a state, I reach out to God in petition to gain strength and seek answers. It is as though the reality of the relationship I have with God produces a tension that never allows me to linger in extremes.

❖ *Faith's Role in Prayers of Petition and Supplication*

The prayer of petition consists partly of faith. The Bible states in Hebrews 11:1, "Now faith is the assurance of things hoped for, the conviction of things not seen." It is not often discussed, but faith plays an important role in what we request. In the heat of making a request, it's difficult to trust. This difficulty is human nature. Faith's role in the prayer of petition is crucial.

After you pray, you would rise from your knees and, in a sense, walk away from the prayer. Do not set your mind against what you prayed but, rather, adopt and maintain an attitude of thanksgiving. Then you will receive an answer to your prayer. There's an old saying: Faith prays the problem once but continues to pray the solution. As things progress and as more information and opportunities become available, these are added to your prayers. For example, a friend of mine who is a priest in Miami experienced something similar to praying for a solution. He and his congregation labored hard and made huge sacrifices to raise enough money to buy land and build a brand new church on it. They found a good location and made the purchase, feeling as though the fulfillment of God's vision was only months away. However, one of the reports returned, stating the land was contaminated due to leaky, underground tanks. The additional work required on the property was huge and expensive, eventually exceeding their timeline and budget. When he learned of the news, he wanted to go in a corner and curl up in the fetal position. So he went to God in prayer. He communicated the problem. After he prayed the problem and got it off his chest, he prayed for a solution. Then, in 2008, I had the great privilege of preaching in his church, which was the fruit of my prayers of petition. It is a beautiful church—the result of a lot of hard work, sacrifice, faith, and prayer. So be not afraid to ask God what you need. State the problem and then start praying for the solution. Matthew 7:7 says, "Ask, and it will be given you; search, and you will find; knock, and the door will be opened for you."

Many have found it helpful to keep a journal chronicling their prayer journeys, as it is beneficial to keep track of how and when God answered your prayers. There are times when the answer is exactly what we prayed for. Then, to our pleasant surprises, there are times when the answer is very different and has exceeded our expectations. Watchman Nee, a leader in the church in China and a political prisoner during the early twentieth century, found himself amazed when he reread his records of prayers. Nee, concerned about the salvation of the people, once wrote the names of 140 people in his prayer journal, and eighteen months later, all but two had become Christians.[3] When we track answered prayers through journals, it serves as a connection, linking us back to the emotions we experienced when we made our request and intercessions. We tend to forget the intensity of the moment as well as our dependence on God during that time; more importantly, we can forget the way in which God answered our calls for help. Keeping a journal will fix this. When we write in a journal, we step back into that moment, albeit not perfectly, and we reconnect with the desperation or uncertainty we had during that time. By doing so, we

---

[3]   Watchman Nee, *A Living Sacrifice*, (Christian Fellowship Publishers, 1972), p.95

can see how God came through for us in the past and we have confidence to depend on him again through prayer.

Then, on the other hand, there are times when the answer to our prayer was a clear no. As Bill Hybels puts it:

> If the request is wrong, God says, "No."
> If the timing is wrong, God says, "Slow."
> If you are wrong, God says, "Grow."
> But if the request is right, the timing is right and you are right, God says, "Go!"[4]

The answer no is more evident when we chronicle our journeys and reflect on them weeks, months, or even years later. Through journaling, we can also see the grace, love, and wisdom that surround the answer. As William Culbertson, the late Reformed Episcopal bishop, once put it, "Keep praying, but be thankful that God's answers are wiser than your prayers!" Therefore, if you take time to write down your prayer in a journal, you will be amazed at the results once you review it, and your faith in God will surely grow.

Once again, we must remember prayer is not a transaction but a relationship. We can never do enough or be good enough for God to answer our prayer based on our goodness. Yet the Bible says we can come to Him boldly in prayer, just as Christ did. Our relationship with God is not like a relationship with an employer, but like that with a parent, as He is our heavenly Father. On the other hand, an employer considers his employees as a means for providing production, so there is a financial obligation. However, God the Father sees us as his children, heirs of his kingdom, and everything is tied to an inheritance that is not tied to what we produce *for* Him but rather who we are in relationship *with* Him. As our relationship with God the Father grows and evolves, so will the nature of our prayers of petition. So, in petition, we need only to ask.

---

[4]   Bill Hybels, *Too Busy Not to Pray*, IVP, p. 74

four

INTERCESSION: TALKING TO GOD ABOUT OTHERS

C rack open the Bible, and you will see, in every one of its books, examples of people who were in dire straits who connected to others in even more desperate circumstances, and they addressed their concern for these ones by pouring their hearts out to God. In the words of Charles Brent, missionary in the Philippines and bishop of Western New York, "Intercessory prayer might be defined as loving our neighbor on our knees." People who pray like this are convinced God can and will do something if they pray. This sort of prayer is known as intercession because we "go to God" or intercede on the behalf of another.

❖ *Intercessory Prayer in the Old Testament*

In Genesis 18:16–33, we witness a powerful example of intercession. Burdened by the knowledge of Sodom's impending destruction, father Abraham moved into action, pouring out his heart to God and expressing concern for his nephew Lot. Caught by proximity, compromised by familiarity and convenience, Lot and his family were living on ground zero of God's imminent wrath. Even though Sodom's destruction would not have had a direct impact on Abraham, he still pled with God, interceding for the deliverance of his nephew and other innocent people who lived there. He asked God to relent in destroying the area six times, negotiating the salvation of fifty possibly righteous ones down to ten. Abraham ran interference between God's wrath and their certain destruction. Abraham interceded for them, leveraging, as Eric Law would describe it, the holy currencies of time, leadership, and relationship to save lives.

We see this in the ministry of Moses, who spoke to God frequently about His people and always pleading Him to show mercy. Frustration was a common emotion for both God and Moses when dealing with the newly emancipated Israelites. Frequent antics, incessant complaining, and constant sabotage were commonplace. In Exodus chapter 32, the children of Israel went as far as to construct a golden calf, worshiping it while Moses was meeting with God on Mount Sinai. This broke God's heart, so much so that He declared to Moses that he planned to disown them and raise up another people. Yet, despite this monumental expression of frustration, Moses pleaded the case of the Israelites to God himself, saying in verse 11, "But Moses implored the Lord his God, and said, "O Lord, why does your wrath burn hot against your people, whom you brought out of the land of Egypt with great power and with a mighty hand?" Moses knew all too well how complicated people could be, but he still loved them enough to speak to God on their behalf.

The heartfelt need to talk to God about a brother's or sister's condition is at the core of intercession. To pray to God for someone's behalf is a true expression of love. It brings to my mind a story from William Willimon, United Methodist Bishop of Northern Alabama, retired. According to Willimon, during oral examinations in the ordination process, one of the examiners became upset when a candidate said one too many times, "I just love people." Exasperated, the examiner, who was a well-seasoned pastor, interrupted the happy-go-lucky candidate and sarcastically asked, "Do you know these people?" Truth be told, the candidate didn't really know those people, not like the experienced pastor who was examining him. The candidate would grow to know them eventually, just as Moses grew to love the unpredictable nation of Israel that traveled with him. Growing to know people can be a mixed bag, full of delight and frustration, laughter and tears, but it can ultimately lead to powerful, well-informed prayers of intercession. One of the marks of true Christian love is to sacrifice time and expend energy in prayer for those around us, regardless of the dominant emotion that we feel while relating to them.

The prophets of old experienced frustration as well while faithfully praying for difficult people. Challenging wayward kings and apathetic people seemed to be a common sight for the likes of Samuel, Elijah, Elisha, Ezekiel, Isaiah, Jeremiah, Amos, and others. They did not have easy jobs. Their proclamations and prophecies were rarely met with welcome. Neither were their people happy to see them when they came for a visit; it was quite the opposite. When King Jehoshaphat recommended consultation of a prophet in 2 Chronicles 18:7, King Ahab said of Micaiah the Prophet, "… I hate him, for he never prophesies anything favorable about me, but only disaster." Moreover, in 1 Samuel 16:4, the King asked the prophet, "Do you come peaceably?" Immediately after Micaiah gave his unfavorable prophecy, he was rewarded with a slap in the face, as seen in 2 Chronicles 18. Just your average frustrating day in a life of an Old Testament prophet.

Despite the personal abuse, mischaracterizations, and blatant disbelief they experienced, these prophets spoke to God about the people and vice versa. For instance, the Prophet Samuel told the people of God not to imitate the other nations and establish a king because God was their king. They did so anyway, causing Samuel's great frustration. When they realized their mistake, they asked Samuel to pray for them. To which he responded, "Moreover as for me, far be it from me that I should sin against the Lord by ceasing to pray for you; …" (1 Samuel 12:23), Samuel knew, as all of Christians should know today, the great importance of continued prayer for those whom we care about, especially when we see them placing themselves in harm's way. We are to pray with great vigor when people seem to be doing everything for the right reasons, and we should pray even harder for them when they have abandoned their commitment to honor God with their choices and actions. Like Samuel, when those we love close their ears to our legitimate and heartfelt concerns, God's ear is open to hearing our concerns for them. To not pray for them would be a sin. This is the mindset of those who believe in the power of intercession.

❖ Intercessory Prayer in the New Testament

The spirit of intercession of intercession active in the New Testament as well. Here intercession is uniquely modeled and reaches the zenith of its impact. After the death and resurrection of Jesus, the most brilliant and charismatic figure of history, a fledgling group of men captured the hearts of many, the ire of some, and imaginations of all with a message of good news to people who formerly had been discriminated against due to their poverty, gender or race. The good news of love, inclusion, and forgiveness issued forth from their every word and action. They expressed God's power. They were clear examples of his grace.

Repeatedly, we read the words of the New Testament calling us to pray. Paul the Apostle directed people to be intercessors, encouraging them to actively engage in conversation with God about those around them. At times, they simply had a knowledge of some for whom they prayed but had never laid eyes on them.

Paul made it clear in his first letter to Timothy, a young and inexperienced pastor in Ephesus, that if Christians were truly committed to prayer, they needed to pray for those in authority (1 Timothy 2:2), whether they refer to those who had a responsibility in the church or to those with political authority over the majority of people. According to Proverbs 21:1, the Bible says that, "The king's heart is a stream of water in the hand of the Lord; he turns it wherever he will." So a very real thing for them was going to God about the person who exercises leadership over them, which meant the emperor himself. And this is interesting. The emperor was considered a god by many. When Paul finished writing the first and second letters to Timothy, Emperor Nero requested that people worship him, offering sacrifices and displays of honor dedicated to his image. Though being an evil man, void of any righteous proclivities, Nero remained the subject of many prayers of intercession. Think of it—this man was the subject of prayer despite the evil things he had done: he had killed his mother, kicked his pregnant wife to death, burned a large section of Rome in 64 AD to clear the way for his golden palace, and then blamed the fire on Christians. To add insult to injury, the man persecuted the Christian community greatly—even burned some of God's elect on stakes to illuminate the night. Evil, deranged, and drunk with power, Nero tore into the church and the Christian community found itself praying for this man. In so doing, they put into practice their Messiah's command to pray for their enemies in Matthew 5:43–45:

> [43] "You have heard that it was said, 'You shall love your neighbor and hate your enemy.' [44] But I say to you, Love your enemies and pray for those who persecute you, [45] so that you may be children of your Father in heaven; for he makes his sun rise on the evil and on the good, and sends rain on the righteous and on the unrighteous.

The spirit of intercession was upon the apostles in such a way that it was part of how they lived and who they were. Jesus's ability to forgive and to pray for his enemies was the very basis for their spiritual formation. While he was hanging on the cross with his open wounds exposed to the dust in the air and the heat of the sun, he spoke the words found in Luke 23:34 to God the Father about those who were crucifying him, "Father, forgive them; for they do not know what they are doing." Jesus was so countercultural that it baffled most people. So to be his disciple means being just as radical in these categories as he was.

Intercession was of such weighty importance that Paul wrote in Romans 8:34:

> Who is to condemn? It is Christ Jesus, who died, yes, who was raised, who is at the right hand of God, who indeed intercedes for us.

So Paul made it clear that the current ministry of the postresurrection and ascension Jesus is one of prayer, describing intercession as his chief activity and responsibility.

> Eventually, Paul found himself working as an intercessor. Every one of his letters began with how he prayed for the churches. In Philippians 1:3–4, he asserts, [3] I thank my God every time I remember you, [4] constantly praying with joy in every one of my prayers for all of you,

Then he reveals the nature of his prayers to the church of Philippi in verses 9–11:

> ⁹ And this is my prayer, that your love may overflow more and more with knowledge and full insight ¹⁰ to help you to determine what is best, so that in the day of Christ you may be pure and blameless, ¹¹ having produced the harvest of righteousness that comes through Jesus Christ for the glory and praise of God.

Similarly, he wrote in Colossians 1:3, "In our prayers for you we always thank God, the Father of our Lord Jesus Christ," Thus, we see this common thread in all his writing. While reviewing events earlier in his life, Paul remembered how he had persecuted the church and made mention of it in 1 Corinthians 15:9 and Galatians 1:13. No doubt, he was struggled with his memories of the stoning of the Stephen. And as a follower of Jesus, Paul found himself on the receiving end of persecution. Paul grew to the point that he interceded for both his allies and adversaries. Paul ultimately grew to promote and practice Jesus's understanding of intercession.

❖ Intercessory Prayer in the Life of the Early Church

Jesus had modeled the intercessory prayer and passed the baton, so to speak, to the apostles who in turn passed it on to the early church fathers. They followed Jesus's example closely in his precious ministry of praying to God for the benefit of others. Polycarp, Irenaeus, Cyprian, John Chrysostom, Ambrose Bishop of Milan, Augustine of Hippo, and of course, the Cappadocian fathers all preached and wrote about the power of an intercessory prayer.

Early church fathers took seriously Paul's words and instruction to a young pastor ministering in the city Ephesus, found in 1 Timothy 2:1–2: "First of all, then, I urge that supplications, prayers, intercessions, and thanksgivings be made for everyone, 2 for kings and all who are in high positions, so that we may lead a quiet and peaceable life in all godliness and dignity."

Highlighting on this passage, Saint Chrysostom wrote, "Thin what it was for those who persecuted, scourged, banished, and slaughtered the Christians, to hear that those whom they treated so barbarously offered fervent prayers to God for them."[5]

These are people who experienced some of the fiercest bouts of persecution. Yet they had the presence of mind and spirit to offer up prayers for those who were in secular power and for their enemies, who were often the same individuals. The spirit of intercession was alive and well in the church. And we are called to do the same.

❖ *Intercession among the Reformers*

Martin Luther was known to have made a bold prayer of intercession for Melanchthon, his assistant, asking God to heal the illness that threatened to take his life. Luther prayed passionately for Melanchthon because he was so vital in Luther's work for the reformation of the church. As it is well known, not only did Melanchthon rise from his bed of affliction and continued working with Luther, he even outlived the great reformer by many years and spoke at his funeral. This is a reminder to the words found in the King James Version of James 5:16: "The effectual fervent prayers of a righteous man availeth much."

This was not exclusive to Luther but to other reformers as well, such as Calvin, Zwingli, Cranmer of the Church of England, and John Knox; they were all mighty intercessors. Knox, for instance, was such a force in prayer that Mary, Queen of Scots, was moved to say, "I fear the prayers of John Knox more than all the assembled armies of Europe."

History shows us that the reformers were not without their flaws, yet they were men who were strong in faith and powerful in intercessory prayer. Like them, we too are faithful but flawed. But, thanks to God, we are also forgiven. They were real people who lived in a time of great pressure, and out of their lives emerged amazing intercession. They prayed for others because they of the wholehearted belief that God acts on the behalf of others when we ask Him.

---

[5] John Chrysostom, *Homily 6 on First Timothy.*

✧ *The Daily Nature of Intercessory Prayer*

Whereas evangelism involves talking to people about God, intercessory prayer is talking to God about people. Interestingly, intercessory prayer is at work in our daily prayers for those who are sick or in need. We have all seen the prayer list and bulletins of our churches and have heard the names of the sick during the service. These people include those went to the hospital, those enduring the regular process of chemotherapy or radiation treatments for cancer, those who have miscarried in pregnancy, the homebound and lonely, and the dying—all who would benefit greatly from every medical advancement that has been made. Through modern technology such as MRIs and CAT scans, we can now see what's going on inside the body from the outside. Yet despite every major advancement in medicine, people still get sick daily. Moreover, death is still upon all of us. Jesus is concerned for his church regarding such matters.

Every Christian is an intercessor who has the responsibility and obligation to speak to God about these people. Much like the prophet Samuel acknowledged his responsibility to pray for the people of Israel, we must also acknowledge our responsibility to pray for those who are sick among us, bringing their cases and situations before the divine throne and asking our holy God to administer His grace and mercy to them in difficult situations. Prayers for the sick and dying do not only reveal the limits of medical science but also highlight how much those who provide care also need the support of prayer. Intercession during these times acknowledges that God is Jehovah Rapha, the Lord and Our Physician. It underscores our great dependence on God.

✧ *Intercessory Prayer and Evangelism*

Prayers of intercession play a vital role in evangelism as well. Praying for the souls of people is also part of the daily intercessory habits of a normal Christian life. It has been said, "No intercession, no evangelism." Among all the affluence and opportunity surrounding us, the church reminds its people of the hunger for greater meaning in life. Since human beings are goal-seeking creatures, they tend to satisfy their specific needs in any way they can—by even throwing things or substances to gratify our spiritual needs. We try to satisfy our desires with accomplishments and material possessions, only to find out how poor they are as substitutes for satisfying those needs. Our deepest spiritual needs can't be sated with material goods.

Intercessory prayer connects us with God's heart and his desire to help people. When we pray for anyone, we place their needs before God. In return, God gives us ideas on how we can help them. We are continuously mindful of both God's desire to touch people and people's need for God's touch. We've also heard countless stories of agnostics or atheists who found themselves in contact with the living God after being on someone's prayer list, completely changing their mind on God's existence and ultimately seeking his will for their lives.

The prayer of intercession becomes the fuel for evangelism. It produces focus, drive, and sense of urgency. When you pray for someone to be open to God, it is not an attempt to control him or her or to force your frame of mind or your way of thinking onto that person. Rather, praying for someone else is an expression of love, a genuine act of concern. When we make request for other people, we are tapping into the very nature of Jesus's attitude in his prayer found in John chapter 17 verse 20, where he said, "I ask not only on behalf of these, but also on behalf of those who will believe in me through their word,"

If we are going to experience renewal, transformation, and evangelism in the churches, it will be in direct proportion to the intercessory prayers made by ordinary Christians. In my early twenties, I worked as a copier technician for a two-year period. One of my copier calls was to a church, and I fell into an interesting conversation with a young man who worked there. He shared his spiritual journey with me, laying out the story of his conversion to Christianity and how he was so overwhelmed about the change he was experiencing internally. It drove him to pray for his family. Soon thereafter, his mother became a Christian, embracing the waters of baptism almost a year after her son did. Something amazing was happening. His dad, however, was the toughest nut to crack. But it only inspired him to be more relentless in prayer. He did so in the spirit found in 1 Thessalonians 5:17, which says only three words: "pray without ceasing,"

Since God is omnipotent, there exists the belief that God will do what He wants regardless if we pray. Yes, God is omnipotent, and He can do whatever He wants, but there are things He will not do unless we pray. Because of the agency God has given us, our prayers play a vital role in how He works in the world. In his sermon on prayer, Alastair Begg compared our role in prayer to the role of a key in a safety deposit box. When you go to the bank to pick up the contents of the safety deposit box, there are two keys that are required to open it. The first is your key, and the second is the bank's. It takes both keys to open that box—one key will not do. Likewise, in prayer, there is the agency of God and the agency of His people, who are responsible to pray on the behalf of others. One will not and cannot work without the other.

In summary, prayer of petition is the first level of intimacy with God, with the second level being intercession. In petition, the vertical beam of the cross is in operation. But in intercession, both the vertical beam (our relationship with God) and the horizontal beam (our relationships with our neighbors) are in motion, and amazing results take place.

five

PRAYER OF PENITENCE

What is the prayer of penitence? Simply put, it refers to confession. We know that confession involves pouring out our hearts and coming clean on what we have done wrong. It sounds clear and simple, but it is not easy to do. When the prayer of penitence takes place, it pulls at all of our resources because it challenges us to change, to look at God differently, and to treat our neighbors in the ways they ought to be treated as well. It requires a lot from us because it calls upon us to look closely at our relationship with the God of creation and take seriously the ministry of his son, Jesus Christ the Lord.

Sin is an interrupter of intimacy and confession addresses it. Have you ever had a conversation with someone after something awkward has taken place? It's difficult to do. You can't have a real conversation when there is an offense between two people. Thus, the air must be cleared. Most of us know from experience that there is no real conversation until we have dealt with the painful thing that was said at the dinner party or slight that happened in public or the letdown caused by a broken promise on the part of a trusted loved one or friend. It is the epitome of a dysfunctional relationship when two people pretend nothing happened or something serious hasn't taken place. Hollywood is full of actors, but our friends and family don't make their living playing roles. No, we're surrounded by real people, actual situations, and genuine hurt. God is not an actor either, which means He will not play along in our games of denial and self-delusion. Rather, He stands as a healthy dose of reality in a sin-sick world of make-believe.

We see this interruption of intimacy all the time. I once opened up and said to a group of men at our church, "I get tired of apologizing to my wife." In response, one of our sage members known for his wisdom and thoughtfulness in relationships, said, "You'd better get used to apologizing to her because you'll be doing it for the rest of your life." Those were sobering words. Yet, they were so true. When we hurt those we love, a rupture in communication usually occurs as well. When this happens, you can cut through the uncomfortable silence with a knife. All of us have experienced this at one time or another in relationships. On a higher level, we all know what it's like to experience distance with God. No real, honest, open conversation can occur until we address the elephant in the room. Knowing this, Jesus said in Matthew 5:23–24:

> [23] So when you are offering your gift at the altar, if you remember that your brother or sister[a] has something against you, [24] leave your gift there before the altar and go; first be reconciled to your brother or sister, and then come and offer your gift.

In other words, straighten things out before you continue any further. The fractured relationship you are ignoring is a hindrance to any religious activities in which you plan to participate in at the altar. In fact, in the eyes of God, our fractured relationships and religious expressions are connected and greatly inform one another.

Penitence lays bare our limitations and allows us to share them with God. Of course, he already knows of them, but we must be vulnerable about our failures and need to have His presence in our lives. There's no pretending with God. He knows all and sees all; he sees exactly what we're going through, as well as our shortcomings, frustrations with others and ourselves. He is also familiar with our hopes, dreams, and desires that keep us getting up every morning and push us to do our best. With all this vital information, He sees us differently and more completely than anyone else. So confessing our sins to Him through the prayer of penitence is serious soul business because all of us reside on the corner of Human Messiness and God's Mercy, and God has answers for this when we come before Him with an honest and sharing heart.

✥ *What are we Confessing?*

It's a question we must seriously consider. Well, the 1979 *Book of Common Prayer* of the Episcopal Church effectively explains what the content of confession truly is. On page 360, it states:

> "We confess that we have sinned against you, in thought, word, and deed, by what we have done and by what we have left undone. We have not loved you with our whole heart. We have not loved our neighbors as ourselves. We are truly sorry and we humbly repent. For the sake of your son Jesus Christ have mercy on us and forgive us our sins as we forgive those who sin against us."

As soon as we encounter this prayer, we focus on the fact that we have " ...sinned in thought, word, and deed ...." This means that sin originates in our thinking and then appears through our words and actions. The Apostle James, the brother of our Lord, addresses this in James 1:14–15:

> [14] But one is tempted by one's own desire, being lured and enticed by it; [15] then, when that desire has conceived, it gives birth to sin, and that sin, when it is fully grown, gives birth to death.

There is also an old secular saying that still holds true: "Things are twice created - first, in thought and, second, in action."

The amazing human mind is the soil for all sorts of grand activity, remarkable kindness, and unthinkable evil. The mind that can compose the genius work like that of Mozart's and Beethoven's or launch the Hubble telescope into space to discover new galaxies and planets is the same one capable of devising schemes and atrocities like those we witnessed in the Armenian genocide, the Holocaust, and the Rwandan genocide, just to name a few.

The Confession from the *Book of Common Prayer* also addresses the potential of sin to be "known" and "unknown." What is a "known" sin? Well, a known sin is deliberate, in which we are aware that we are offending God. In other words, we are conscious of the sins we commit, and we bear the responsibility for it. In the Bible, we can read examples of known sins in Genesis 4:1–16, when Cain's murdered his brother Abel; in 2 Samuel 11, when King David abused his power, as he bore the rotten fruit of adultery and murder; and in Matthew 2:16–18, when Herod's issued the fear-inspired command to mass murder all male children aged two and younger. In modern times, there exist examples of known sins: Jeffrey Dahmer's cannibalistic murders; Dylan Klebold's shooting of unarmed African-Americans during a Bible study in South Carolina; Bernie Madoff's active role in destroying people's lives, leaving them penniless through his Ponzi scheme; a police office kneeling on the neck of George Floyd until life left his body. These people knew exactly what they were doing; thus, these people knew their sin.

On countless occasions, people have suffered torture, discrimination, and dehumanization. Anytime there is a case of human trafficking, there is usually someone involved who has complete knowledge of the situation. They are fully aware of the wrong they have committed. We can try to blame someone else for sins or attribute our bad deeds to evil forces beyond our control, but in the end, we must take responsibility of them. When I was a child, my family used to enjoy the Flip Wilson Show. Regularly, Flip Wilson would dress in drag and play the role of a woman named Geraldine. And every time Geraldine was caught doing something wrong, she would say, "The devil made me do it." In the same sense, we can't get away with our sins simply by saying that. Rather, the scriptures and the confessions of Christian tradition make it clear that we are to take responsibility for our actions. So we must be honest about our failures and sins. We are called to confess and amend our ways to set a new path with our lives.

On the other hand, "unknown" sins are a complicated and difficult matter. Throughout history, there have been people who have been complicit in specific sins or sins against humanity but were never fully aware of what they were doing. There were even normal, everyday things people did that would make all of us cringe now. Within the last 100 years, people used to do things like put their children in outdoor baby cages, smoke during pregnancy, send babies through the mail, and visit mental hospitals for entertainment. And we haven't even addressed the more egregious sins surrounding race and gender. Yes, we can point fingers at the people from the past and point out their sins, but it will also be the case that in the future others will point out the many sins of our time. We might not even be aware of them now. But rest assured that someday and somehow, currently unknown sins will come to light. We can't escape from it. Therefore, it would be wise to exercise humility. Just think—200 years from now, an entire nation or perhaps even the entire world, might point their fingers at us, saying, "How could those folks have done this or that back then?." I guarantee it. For that reason, as the future will clearly reveal the sins of our era, we need to confess right now for the sins of which we are not even conscious presently.

❖ A Biblical Example of Penitence

Daniel stood in prayer for the nation of Israel, a nation experiencing of captivity and exile. Having the best and brightest of their people stripped away from them, there was only a remnant left and Jerusalem had to start over. They lacked people resources necessary to make it. With their most talented and able people taken away from them, this remnant was left to its own devices in a desperate attempt to restore Jerusalem, not to what it once was but simply to the point where it was safe and functional. In response to reports of his people's dire circumstances, a young man named Daniel who was held in Babylonian captivity prayed to God about the situation of His people. A major part of his prayer consisted of penitence. He was grieved, and he expressed great sorrow with what had taken place with Israel. He confessed the shortcomings and sins of his nation, which were committed well before his birth. Although he was not directly involved in the sins of Israel's the past, he confessed their sins as though he shared responsibility by saying, "we sinned" rather than "they sinned." Thus, he took part in the blame and responsibility for sins he did not commit.

Daniel's confession serves as a pre-Christian example of the kind of spiritual posture that penitence can develop within a follower of Jesus. It connects us with others in a way that we don't sit in condescending judgement of the people of the past, but rather we seek to join them in the fold of our common humanity, acknowledging that other people's sins are our sins too. I can recall a time when I heard about the crucifixion of Jesus years ago. The question was asked, "Who killed Jesus? The Jews or the Romans?" I will never forget the answer: "They both did. In reality, we killed him as well—you and I—and we continue to do so daily in many ways."

❖ Sin Committed on Our Behalf

Penitence is needed for sins committed on our behalf. It is part of the human condition, and the church goes as far as to address it in one of the alternative confessions of sin, which to state: "We repent of the evil that enslaves us, the evil we have done, and the evil done on our behalf."[6]

We benefit from someone else's misery and hardship. When Chinese workers at Foxconn jumped to their deaths in a wave of suicides in 2010 and 2011, we must acknowledge how we benefited from their misery, because their plight guaranteed us affordable iPhones. In many cases, even children have been exploited, just so we can have what we have. The end game of companies is to keep expenses cheap, but at what price—human lives? There always seems to be another human life attached to the benefits and conveniences we enjoy in life. When we look around us, we can see the extent of how others have been exploited and sinned against just for our well-being. It is likely that we will repent for this generation, not merely for its vitriolic words and the violent actions of bad people, but also for the appalling silence and indifference of the good people who sit around and say, "Wait, it's not time."

❖ Restitution

Restitution is to the prayer of penitence what teeth are to a mouth. Without teeth, we cannot chew food and eventually swallow it to have the necessary nourishment for our bodies. This is the major error that most of us make;

---

[6]   Early Fathers prayers ~ research

we may have the desire of penitence but without restitution. Restitution refers to the act of turning back from our ways and making up for what you have done. Do you believe you have a moral obligation to pay back what you have taken or to make right what you have made wrong?

Over the years, there's been a lot of talk about cheap grace. But when confession connects with restitution, cheap grace will not even exist. An example of restitution is when a thief is heartbroken over his sin that he confesses and returns what he has taken. Restitution can also refer to fixing the damage we may have caused to someone's reputation by publicly retracting our statements and apologizing for our words. Restitution involves trying to correct the wrongs of the past by providing opportunities for people whom we have abused, marginalized or victimized over the years. Restitution recognizes that an apology is empty when it is not supported by actions or attempts to make things right. If an eight-year-old child drops a bowl of ice cream on the floor, makes a mess, and apologizes for it, the child's parents will accept the apology, but they will likely also say, "Now, please clean it up!" Both the apology and subsequent cleaning are combined to produce restitution. Without both, it is not true penitence.

In her book *Daniel Deronda*, George Eliot wrote, "No evil dooms us hopelessly except the evil we love, and desire to continue in, and make no effort to escape from."

Moving away from evil with acts of contrition and restitution is part of the 'effort to escape' from the control of evil. It gives teeth to our prayer when we confess our sins to God. We must make up for the damage caused by our actions and inaction, our careless words and cowardly silence, and resolve to rectify the situation.

❖ *Penitence as Spiritual Posture*

When we were younger, how often were we told that good posture is important? Our parents and teachers would tell us to, "Stand up straight! Arch your back! Don't slouch!" Their efforts to coach us on proper posture went beyond the good impression and entered the realm of health. Posture is the body's relationship with the ever-present reality of gravity. So, if our spines aren't aligned properly, our physical health will pay for it. Head, neck, and shoulder—even digestion and breathing—are influenced greatly by poor posture. The lack of good posture increases stress and depression. Similarly, spiritual posture has a profound effect on us as well. It is our relationship to the truth of God. Anger, depression, delusion, blaming, ongoing guilt, inability to forgive others and oneself, are all the results of poor spiritual posture. But instead of telling us to stand up straight and avoid slouching, our tradition addresses spiritual posture by urging us to continually be honest with God through confession and to turn from anything that takes us out of fellowship with him and with our neighbor, otherwise known as repentance and restitution[7]. If we fail to do this, the spiritual help we wish to receive will become compromised. The results of the prayer of penitence and the concomitant act of contrition are important for the spiritual posture of every Christian.

❖ *Spiritual Calibration*

Every day, thousands of people test their blood sugar on blood sugar meters. These people are depending the accuracy of these meters in order to properly care of their illness, but doctors and medical specialists will tell you that many of them out of calibration, some as much as 20%. William Lee Dubois, an Endocrinology Diabetes and Metabolism specialist, noted that he has seen mis calibrated meters that were as much as 100 to 150 points off. This is far more than being just slightly off; this is dangerously off. It may even be life-threatening.[8]

Penitence not only corrects our spiritual posture; it can calibrate the soul. In machinery, calibration involves detecting the current state of a machine and bringing it back it's set standard. Granted, human beings are not machines but rather, they are God's creation with a distinct purpose we can't avoid. To achieve God's purpose for us, we need fine-tuning. When our souls lack calibration, everything is off, and we get out of touch with God's mission, Christ's love, and God's purpose for our lives.

What is this "soul" in need calibration? Sometimes, there is a bit of confusion about the soul. In scripture, there are places where the terms

---

[7]   Enriching Our Worship 1, page 56, Church Publishing Incorporated

[8]   Share.com

"spirit" and "soul" are used interchangeably. For instance, Genesis 41:8 points out that following his dreams, Pharaoh's 'spirit' was troubled. In the gospels, John 12:27 mentions how Jesus was troubled in his 'soul', then troubled in his 'spirit' in John 13:21. In these instances, "spirit" and "soul" seem to communicate the same thing. However, there are other places in scripture where there is a distinct difference between soul and spirit. In those instances, the soul refers to a combination of the mind, will, and emotions of a Christian.

Given this definition of the soul, what does it means for us to be calibrated to the heart of God? We are encouraged to follow the mind of Christ, but we don't always think like him. However, adjusting ourselves through scripture, prayer, and proper relationships will calibrate us where we should be spiritually. Because his life and mind are the standard, our will and desires need to be adjusted to meet it. When his will and our desires are finally aligned, we are then fulfilling the will of God. For that to be a continuous experience, we must be attuned to him. Similarly, what we love intensely must be in conjunction with what he loves intensely. We can't say we hate people but love Jesus, because he didn't hate people. For our emotions to be calibrated to his, we must love what he loves, value what he values, mourn what he mourns, hate what he hates, and rejoice in what brings him joy.

When life is spiritually calibrated through true confessional prayer, penitence ceases to be seen as a time when God calls us to put the brakes on our bad behavior. Instead, it serves as a tool to be used for continued faithfulness. Once, I heard the Rt. Reverend Nathan Baxter, a retired Episcopal Bishop of the Diocese of Central Pennsylvania, discuss the hound dog and how it tracks. By sniffing back-and-forth within a range, he explained, the animal can track the scent by sensing where it isn't as much as it senses where it is. The hound dog is always recalibrating his sense of smell by staying connected to the source of the scent, because that is the standard. I am not comparing Christians to dogs, but there is a lesson to be learned in this example. God's people must be focused to always pick up the scent of the Spirit of God, always discerning where it is and isn't. This sort of 'tracking' will never veer us off course.

Over 1600 years ago, Ambrose, of Milan, penned this prayer of penitence:

O Lord, who hast mercy upon all, take away from me my sins,
and mercifully kindle in me the fire of thy Holy Spirit.
Take away from me the heart of stone,
and give me a heart of flesh,
a heart to love and adore thee,
a heart to delight in thee,
to follow and to enjoy thee,
for Christ's sake.
(Ambrose of Milan, c. 339–397)

six

PRACTICE OF PRAYER

◈ *Prayer Routine*

He walked several miles every day. He started with the same destination in mind every day. He wasn't driven by the desire to stay in shape or to hear the birds singing while he strolled along. Instead, Ralph Waldo Emerson meandered the same route routinely to visit the grave of his deceased wife, Ellen. He was overwhelmed by the loss of her, and as he would make his way to her grave, he carried on long conversations with her spirit. It was his routine.[9] As unusual as it may sound to us, this was a habit common among people in Emerson's day. Many surviving spouses made similar grief walks. It was an important habit in their process of grief. Such repetition kept the memory and relationship they'd had with their deceased spouses alive.

A routine of prayer might be unappealing to some. Others prefer to think of praying as an overwhelming desire to talk with God. Most do not think of it as being calendar bound or scheduled like a doctor's appointment. We wish for it to be spontaneous, passionate, and always a fresh experience. However, most often, it doesn't work that way. You see, to speak of prayer in these times is to come to terms of a routine that involves relationship, rhythm, and full engagement.

---

[9]   Emerson: The Mind on Fire, Robert D. Richardson

Daily habits are important. The most basic habits, such as using a toothbrush or making the bed to checking in with children or seeing about the condition of aging parents, have a profound effect.

The daily habit of prayer is essential. The Psalmist proclaimed in Psalm 63:

O God, thou art my God; early will I seek thee:
my soul thirsteth for thee,
my flesh longeth for thee in a dry and thirsty land,
where no water is.

For the Psalmist, he sought not only daily, but early.

There are some tools that can help us commit to this habit. In most Christian religions, there is some sort of prayer office and a regular time to come before the Lord. These are prayers developed to help people make it through their days. In my denomination, the Episcopal Church, the following prayers are part of our daily routine: morning prayer, noonday prayer, evening prayer, and compline prayer. Other denominations have similar schedules, designed to keep people engaged in praying to God.

When I was first ordained in the ministry, I arrived at a parish that practiced daily morning and evening prayer. Early on, I thought these prayers were simply an addendum to the day, a simple add-on. You know, something that is nice to do. Rather, it was its foci, punctuating our life together, serving as the pivot points for the parish's ministry. It was so important that all our appointments and hospital visits were scheduled around the prayer times. Often, I would find myself rushing away from the bedside of a sick parishioner at the hospital, knowing I only had fifteen minutes to make it in time for evening prayer. However, such a routine created a rhythm and filled the day with meaning. Those prayer times put the day in its place, making it clear to everyone that it was a priority. As a result, I grew from that experience, for we stuck with the same practice through the terrorist attacks of 9/11, elections, and other significant local and global events. Those events, as tragic and as wonderful as some were, they were all framed by prayer, by the daily routine of conversation with God.

The act of seeking isn't exclusive to professionals—it can apply to every believer. In the Lord's Prayer, it says, "Give us this day our daily bread." This is a clear indication that asking is to be done regularly as well. In other words, we could say, "I needed help from you in the past, and you gave it to me. I need provisions for today, and I trust that you are giving them to me. And I will most likely have a great need in the future, and I am confident in your ability to make it happen then as well." It's our way of saying how much we trust God with the known and with the yet-to-be known. As one popular saying goes: "I may not know what the future holds, but I know who holds the future." Truly, God is the one who holds the future. God is the "the ground of being," as Paul Tillich used to put it, and all power is in His hand. With this in mind, we routinely seek Him.

The apostles of the church recognized prayer as the foundation of a relationship. They knew instinctively that prayer was not words punctuated by silence but rather silence punctuated by words. For them, prayer was a way of being, a state of the new creation, so to speak. In Acts chapter 7, the apostles decided to commit themselves to a daily routine of study, seeking God through prayer.

This routine is based on the need for a daily habit and the results it produces. We understand the necessity for prayer; it is as important as the air we breathe, and its daily intake is essential for life. It wasn't until I was fifty that I became aware of how important it was to have a good diet. There were some things that I could no longer eat—well, I could eat them, but I would pay for it and later feel sluggish and sick. I paid attention to my diet not because it was the fashionable thing to do but because my health and vitality depended on it. I found eating well necessary in order to just make it through the day. Plus, the results were amazing. Simply eating more vegetables and reducing my intake of greasy food made a difference. Lord knows I love greasy food. However, the impact of just limiting my intake made all the difference in the world. I had more energy. I felt better throughout the day. I didn't have to consume as much caffeine to make it through the afternoon. My diet, my eating routine, made a difference and produced results. Our prayer routines can bear similar results in a spiritual sense. Consistent prayer brings us closer to God, generates understanding and empathy, and accomplishes more than we could ever imagine. We have all experienced it personally or have heard from other people how prayer and devotional reading starts the day off on the right tone.

Most people find themselves jumping into their conversations with God in a state of urgency or emergency. The impulse to bombard God with our needs in media res (in the middle), without any background or relationship, is natural but not ideal. In a state of urgency or emergency, the strong and seemingly self-contained have dropped to their knees and pleaded God for help, "Lord, please just get me through this." All of us have done it at one time or another and will continue to do so. However, it is entirely different thing to approach God with our emergency when we already have an ongoing routine that sustains us over a long period of time. For instance, in Acts 16:25–31, when Paul and Silas found themselves in a jail in Philippi, their prayers rose from desperate circumstances, but it was also part of their daily routine of prayer. Such a prayer even bore fruit, with the conversion of a Philippian jailor.

❖ Aids to Prayer

Written Prayers

He stared at me in pain and confusion. And I had no idea what to do, except what my rector had instructed over the phone from the night before. My rector would have been there himself, but he was out of state on church business. I was this man's second option. As I stood next to his bed, fumbling through the pages of the *Book of Common Prayer*, I reached my hand to take his. With sunken eyes and shriveling skin on his bones, he wanted to communicate something to me, but no words came out—only grunts of desperation. He was facing the last hours of his long fight with bone cancer. It had metastasized throughout his body, eventually entering his brain, until that moment when we were face-to-face. I would be the last clergyperson he would ever see, and he was the first parishioner for whom I ever said final prayers prior to death.

Words eluded me. I didn't know what to say, but the *Book of Common Prayer* became my resource, equipping me with words when I had none. It defined my time with him and honored the man in his final hours.

Although praying for that dying man was over twenty years ago, I can still remember his face as if it were yesterday. There are times when we want to communicate with God, but words escape us, times when we don't know what to say or what to pray. Grasping smoke would have been easier than grasping for such words. We may experience things in life that may be too tragic or painful for words to describe, and we need other resources to help us with this process. The passing of a loved one, the death of a child, the emotional rawness in the aftermath of terrorism, or so many other things, all make it difficult to communicate our feelings when we go through them. When we know we should pray and we want to pray but cannot find the words, written prayers can be a resource to help us. These written prayers can help us process our new realities and open us up to things we may have overlooked.

Sometimes, as with any insight, what is revealed is our reluctance to accept that we need the resources of our spiritual tradition more than we are willing to admit. As a young Christian, I was quite critical of written prayers and anyone who would recite them publicly. I judged the practice as an overreliance on a request authored by another person and, therefore, a lack of real spirituality. I took pride in not needing those prayers, and believed they were used as a crutch for those who knew nothing—or at best, very little—about the Spirit of God. Boy, I was wrong. Now, I find myself taking great comfort in written prayers, marveling at their thoughtfulness and sheer genius in getting to the heart of the matter. It's not that I trust my extemporaneous prayers less than the prayers of saints of the past. I just trust their prayers increasingly more as the years go by. Most of all, I trust their frank conversations with God and how they are respectfully and thoughtfully composed around similar issues I may have. In the same way that the disciples asked Jesus how to pray and he gave them what we know as the Lord's Prayer, the disciple in me asks the Jesus in those who have gone before me to teach me how to talk to God about a specific matter, and I receive the answer through their written prayers.

The prayers of the saints are powerful in that they get to the heart of the matter, they expose our desires and reservations, and they move us closer to an understanding. Again, the prayers of the saints are powerful in that they put us in touch with God, and nudge us to pursue a more honest existence, because honesty was first modeled in their prayer. The prayers of the saints also help with soul searching. They give us the license and confidence to pray more, showing us how to voice concerns that have previously gone unsaid.

I remember the first time I stumbled over the Prayer for the Sanctification of Illness in the *Book of Common Prayer*. I was stunned by it, for it addressed a messiness I often considered, and it dared to grapple with terminal illness. It enhanced my trust in God and how He can be profoundly present at the time of death.

Let's look at it together:

> Sanctify, O Lord, the sickness of your servant, that the sense of his weakness may add strength to his faith and seriousness to his repentance; and grant that he may live with you in everlasting life; through Jesus Christ our Lord. Amen.

When we think that God has abandoned us, a prayer like this allows us to see the reality of his presence, and we feel secure in knowing he is intimately involved in our lives. I cannot recall how many times I prayed this prayer with those who were preparing to pass through the veil that separates the temporal from the eternal. The prayer relieved the ill and comforted the supporting family.

When Harry Emerson Fosdick was a seminarian, he suffered a nervous breakdown. Since then, he led a life of prayer that empowered him for the duration of his ministry and sustained him for the rest of his life. When reading his book of prayers, one cannot help but feel his vulnerability. Fosdick opened his soul and completely exposed himself in his prayers.

In his book, *The Meaning of Prayer*, Fosdick states, "Prayer is not growing after him. Prayer is opening life up to him. The prayer-less heart is fleeing from God. Finding God is letting him find us; for a search for him is simply surrender to the search for us. When this truth is clearly seen, prayer becomes real."[10]

Fosdick captured what it is to talk to God. The sense of searching and being found is at the heart of prayer. Fosdick was empowered with a sense of what it is to pursue God in prayer. When we pray Fosdick's prayers, we become collaborators in this pursuit. When Fosdick's prayers are recited, one feels closer to God and His love and mercy. Fosdick's prayers transcend petitions because they become important exchanges with

---

[10] The Meaning of Prayer, page 87, Harry Emerson Fosdick, TheClassics.us

the divine, instead. These deep and meaningful discussions are like the muffled tones of conversations with those who, even though they exceed us in wisdom, still give us time because of their great affection for us.

So when we open the vault of our concerns and find more troubles than words can express, these prayers come to our assistance. Whether they are the litanies of Lancelot Andrewes, John Wesley, Harry Emerson Fosdick, or others, we find ourselves comforted by what they express.

❖ *Prayer and Reading the Narratives in Scriptures*

Praying is special. Consider this: in prayer, we have the opportunity talk with the Creator of the universe. In our conversations with God, do we honestly disclose all our fears, express our hopes and dreams, and demonstrate love for others through intercession? This can all take place when we talk to God.

When we dare to talk with Him, we tap into a divine frequency, tune our channels to God's divine channel, and become open to His sacred broadcast.

As much as I believe praying is special, I believe that praying while reading scripture is even more so. I was introduced to it by several ministers in the early 1990s. Some of them had very strong impacts on me, and they inspired me to pray more and ignited a passion within me for a deeper spiritual life. Those ministers exposed me to a new way of reading scripture, which remains with me to this day. Yet it was learning about prayer, coupled with scripture reading, that inspired me the most. This was entirely new to me. Since I was a serious student of the Bible, I would devote my time to entire sections and would enhance the experience with the help of commentaries. In this way, merging prayer with my Bible reading exposed me to a new dimension. To put it bluntly, I was hooked.

Going back and forth with God while reading the Bible was like knowing the mind of God. I felt His love for me and the world. I felt my prayers expressing His priorities and concerns back to Him. Talking to God while reading the scripture helped me connect with God even more. In each biblical character, I saw a little of myself. Not only did the passages speak to my situation, but to the situations and circumstances of people who were close to me.

❖ *Praying Through the Powerful Stories of the Bible*

Praying the scriptures comes in a few forms. The first is through the engaging stories of holy writ and looking for the dominant lessons and emotions in them.

Some stories promote courage, while others promote long-suffering and endurance in the face of overwhelming odds and seemingly impossible circumstances. Still, others communicate the power of teamwork and what can take place when people pool their resources and define their goals.

Praying through the scripture can simply mean seeking God's mind regarding the wisdom we need to gain from the stories of the Bible. For example, consider the story in 2 Samuel 24:1–25, when King David made sacrifices on the threshing floor of Araunah the Jebusite. David had decided to take a census, looking to see how many fighting men he had in both Judah and Israel. The overall tone of the passage implies that it is not right to do such a thing. Joab, David's most trusted general, attempted to dissuade him from doing it, but David used the weight of his office and position to push his plan forward. And that's what he did. He discovered he had eight hundred thousand fighting men in Israel and five hundred thousand fighting men in Judah—men who would sacrifice their lives for their king and country. After David counted the men, verse 10 tells us this:

> But afterward, David was stricken to the heart because he had numbered the people. David said to the Lord, "I have sinned greatly in what I have done. But now, O Lord, I pray you, take away the guilt of your servant; for I have done very foolishly."

The text does not reveal it, but based on our knowledge of human nature, we can be quite sure King David thought the following before he came to his woeful realization recorded in verse 10.

Great, he probably thought. *I have an army totaling 1.3 million men. With such a formidable force, I can take on anyone and any nation.* It's likely he derived confidence from that number. However, it was entirely the wrong move. It was misplaced assurance. Then he probably realized what he had done and how it wasn't worth it. So the death angel of the Lord came against all of Israel, delivering a horrible plague, which ultimately killed seventy thousand men, women, and children in just three days.

So David went to the threshing floor of Araunah the Jebusite and made a sacrifice to avert any additional distraction. When David offered to pay for the threshing floor, Araunah offered to give it to him for free. In response, in verse 24, David resisted, saying, "No, but I will buy them from you for a price; I will not offer burnt offerings to the Lord my God that cost me nothing." When I first read this story, that statement by David pierced my heart and brought me to my knees. I had to inspect the very nature of my daily life before God, and consider the price I am willing to pay, and it helped me question whether I was looking for something that would cost me nothing. Because of that experience was bathed in prayer, I share that passage of scripture with every new class I teach at our parish. For me, it is important for them to take their faith journey seriously, to never settle for sacrificing something that would cost them nothing.

Another example is the account of Jacob wrestling with God in Genesis 32:22–32. He had hurt a lot of people, especially his brother Esau. Scripture tells us that he was anxious about running into his brother, and for good reason. He had cheated his brother out of his birthright and, therefore, changed the direction of his life. Jacob was nervous about the meeting, especially after finding out that his brother was coming with four hundred men. With great anxiety, he anticipated his impending encounter with Esau, so he sent gifts ahead of him to help his cause. Then, the night before meeting his brother, Jacob had an encounter. "When the man saw that he did not prevail against Jacob, he struck him."

If we allow it, we can enter prayerful reflection on Jacob's wrestling and through it come face-to-face with our own tendencies to seek instant resolution. It's an opportunity to explore the tension between the hope of our faith and the everyday problems we encounter. When this tension is honestly explored, we often see that the resolution is not instant. The messy stuff of life fails to be wrapped up and resolved like a murder investigation on the old TV show *Columbo*. Life and the conditions of life are far more complex than anything television can offer. Those little points in life tend to be the ongoing mat on which we wrestle. If we're honest, we go from having the problem pin us, to us pinning the problem, to only finding ourselves pinned down again. As one of my clergy colleagues said when expressing his exhaustion in the process of struggling with God, "I'm way past the point of having my hip dislocated in this wrestling match with God. I've been wrestling for a long time." One thing that marks Jacob's strength and growth is the fact that he didn't resolve things immediately after he went through them.

Jacob's name means "deceiver" in Hebrew. Among ancient peoples, one's name represented one's character. Jacob was in a fight with everyone and everything since the day of his birth. Even though most of his problems came from his character defects, he continued to benefit from his bad behavior, all in the pursuit of getting what he wanted. When this is the case, necessary changes are hard to come by because the incentive for changing is not there. Likewise, if we continue to operate in our dysfunction while reaping a seeming benefit, what will prompt us to change, even if a change is in our best interest? So something had to take place to fulfill God's future for him. A God-oriented wrestling match had to be part of it.

Deep in the soul of every person, there is a vigorous grappling that takes place with the almighty God. We find ourselves grappling with all that we are called to be and struggling with all that we are called to avoid. All that we are and all that we're not is involved in this wrestling match.

This wrestling match is an exercise in brutal honesty. It is a struggle that takes place at the intersection of faith and doubt, the corner of our best and worst selves, the place where the responsible adult and petulance child in us square off and fight for dominance. In her book *Scared by Struggle, Transformed by Hope*, Joan Chittister captured the essence of this reality with these words, "Jacob does what all of us must do if, in the end, we too are to become true. He confronts in himself the things that are wounding him, admits his limitations, accepts his situation, rejoins the world, and moves on." The Scottish theologian, Peter Taylor Forsyth, put it this way: "There is no reality without wrestling, as without the shedding of blood there is no remission [of sin]" (*Minister's Prayer Book*, pg. 384).

In reading scripture and praying through Jacob's story, we see the individual wrestling of this biblical personality.

Biblical narratives serve to remind us how God bears us up under the weight of life's overwhelming situations. In the book of Daniel, we consider Daniel and his companions. We encounter four young men, separated from the community in Israel, who are shoved into captivity in sixth century BC Babylon, and forced to embrace not only an alien land but also an alien lifestyle as well. Ultimately, in such an environment, their integrity came under fire. King Nebuchadnezzar, incensed by the refusal of the Hebrew boys to worship his golden image, threatened to throw them into a furnace of fire for their insolence. So the three young men, supported only by their faith, refused to worship any god or image other than the true God of Israel. According to Daniel 3:23–30, the king had all three men thrown in the fiery furnace, promising them a toasty fate. But something amazing and mind-blowing happened: the awaiting fire did not consume them. Everyone can relate to this because all of us have encountered flames that threatened to consume us. They may not be literal fires, but all of us have faced times when the heat of life has been turned up on us, often to unbearable levels. Yet for every fiery furnace we face in life, the power of prayer prevails and sustains us.

Maintaining integrity was an issue for Meshach, Shadrach, and Abednego, not because someone was monitoring their behavior nor because they were trying to make an impression on the king, but because of their constant contact with God through prayer that made it matter. By their spiritual intimacy, they were living for an audience of one. Their lives were void of the spiritual clutter that seems to overtake most people's mental, emotional, and psychic spaces. In reading the experience of what they went through, we can focus on the energy in it, which causes us, if we allow it, to reexamine our focus and reevaluate our priorities. Prayer, combined with scripture, leads us in asking some hard questions as we approach God. "Am I as committed as they were? Am I seeking to be a person of integrity in every situation?" Eventually, these move from being questions of one's self, to questions directed to God, evolving from the shallow state of self-talk to the deeper state of God talk. I believe these are the types of deep prayers that were on the very breath of the great preacher Harry Emerson Fosdick as he rose from the abyss of his nervous breakdown and depression and took hold of the new life God had for him in Jesus Christ. His prayers were well-worn, like the rugged wood of an old barn, for which newness is a distant memory, its chipping paint only conveys utility. But then, a new beauty emerges. Over time, its structural integrity and utility become its chief characteristic. I also believe that these are the types of heartfelt, passionate prayers that emitted from the soul of Dietrich Bonhoeffer. A mixture of fear and faith and trust fueled his prayers in the final days before his execution by the Nazis. His prayers, like the actions and intentions of the Hebrew boys, dripped with integrity.

What the narratives do for us is akin to Erich Sthick's assertion that right preaching must have *vox humana* and *vox celestia*, that is, human voice and divine voice. When these two voices are in balance, there is transformation. Although he addressed preaching, we can also apply it the biblical narrative's role in helping us pray. In meditating on them, they show us how God embraces the necessity of wrestling in prayer, one which includes the human voice and the divine voice—the voice from below and the voice from above, locking horns. We find the tension between these voices very active in the ministry of Jesus's teaching and praying. Our praying must, therefore, include the rawness of the following present realities: mass shootings, political turmoil, economic and racial discrimination, sexual harassment, fractured relationships, celebrations, and deep regrets. In addition, it should include the voice of divine confidence and providence, the voice from above, the voice that seeks to love one's neighbor as oneself, all of which involves a great deal of messiness. What comes from above is to, as Sthick puts it, "see things as God sees them." In other words, to see things from below is to see them at ground level, while seeing things above is to see them from thirty thousand feet. When this happens, we see differently. We see lives transformed, healing taking place, and forgiveness practiced. The incarnation is an example of that meeting in the middle. The cross, as well, was a self-giving example of it.

At the end of it all, prayer emerges from the reading of scripture like heat emerges from a flame. In reading the words, we hear His voice, and the natural response to hearing God is to speak back to him—to pray. Julius Schniewind captured this perfectly when he wrote, "This listening passes over inevitably into prayer." Scripture reading and prayer become the great cause and effect of our Christian existences, inviting us to walk through new corridors of the conversation with God, one pulling the other into deeper experiences of divine response. Hopefully, in its fullest expression, this will take us into divine surrender.

❖ *Praying the Principles Found in Holy Scripture*

Another part of prayer and scripture is how balancing the two helps us engage and apply biblical principles to our lives. The letters of the apostles are simply letters written to the churches, encouraging everyone to stay consistent with what the apostles taught them while the apostles were with them. Reminding them of familiar principles, the letters reinforced those principles by mentioning the principles in the letters, promoting a culture that took those principles seriously.

You see, the principles of the early church were antithetical to the norms of the culture in which they lived. Strength through weakness, ongoing and limitless forgiveness, an outright rejection of vengeance, the requirement to love one's enemies, and total allegiance to an executed Jewish rabbi over and above any honor given to the emperor were all core principles of Jesus's movement in its early stages. In a nutshell, this lifestyle and ethos were not only countercultural but also downright subversive.

The early church, without question, was a subculture, which made high demands on its members. The sheer weight, responsibility, and risk shielded the community from any infiltration by low-commitment individuals. To be part of the Jesus movement meant putting your life on the line. So the apostles continuously communicated messages that reinforced these original teachings, not to weaken the teaching but to amend it, making them stronger and more robust as time went on. Week after week, Sunday after Sunday, these principles were part of the moral, intellectual, and spiritual diet of the people. These principles made them different and peculiar people in their time, and their nonbelieving neighbors took note.

So let's look at some of these principles that both formed and transformed the lives of the early church by first looking at forgiveness. The leader of their faith, Jesus, had a great many things to say about forgiveness.

❖ *Forgiveness*

One of the most difficult things for us to get our heads around is the biblical concept of forgiveness. Forgiveness stretches us, and when we think we have it down, it eludes us. Forgiveness marked the ministry of Jesus, and to this day, people are completely bewildered by his capacity to do so, given the magnitude of the offense he forgave. He forgave his murderers. His forgiveness extended beyond their singular transgression two thousand years ago and covers the sins we committed yesterday and the ones we will commit tomorrow.

Prayer and forgiveness go together. Granted, we hear stories about people's willingness to forgive. As with any story about forgiveness, whether they are religious or not, I always find myself impressed with what I hear. However, when I hear stories about people who have forgiven without the association of the power of prayer, I have some doubts about the ongoing ability to sustain such an attitude. I make this statement knowing all too well how we can sincerely say we forgive but take it back in action and attitude. The careless words of a friend, the undermining actions of a coworker, the physical abuse of your daughter by the hands of her husband or boyfriend weigh heavy on us. During the day, we thought we had forgiven, but as we lie in our beds in the darkness of the night, staring at the ceiling, completely worn out and unable to sleep, we become acutely aware of how we haven't forgiven. The more we decide to rely on our own power to forgive, the more frequent and intense these sleepless episodes become. You see, the necessity of having the work of forgiveness supported by prayer is indispensable.

Jesus possessed a robust version of forgiveness, which required a great deal more from his followers. For everyone who considers themselves to be subjects of his kingdom, Jesus increased the intensity. His insistence on forgiveness started to be a point of concern for his disciples. They were so concerned about it that they eventually asked him what he considered to be the limits of forgiveness—the cutoff point at which to practice forgiveness would be to practice foolishness. Matthew 18:21–22, deals with this question:

²¹Then Peter came and said to him, "Lord, if another member of the church sins against me, how often should I forgive? As many as seven times?" ²²Jesus said to him, "Not seven times, but, I tell you, seventy-seven times.

For Peter, seven times was good enough. It was the maximum number the rabbis said was permissible before someone could finally decide to cut off the offender. Jesus, however, presented a very different vision of forgiveness, one inextricably linked to how his people would deal with one another. Not considering its limits, Jesus placed a premium on forgiveness because he placed a premium on human relationships. In an era of disposable relationships and cheap life, much like our own, Jesus set a countercultural alternative before them. Yet for it to take hold, prayer needed to have a deep and abiding role.

So to combine prayer and scripture reading is to combine prayer and forgiveness. As impossible as it is to do a perfect number of times, through prayer and reliance upon the power of the Holy Spirit, we can do it. To be moved by this principle in scripture, we must go to God, relying on the power greater than ourselves, one that flows through our lives at the most critical points of our existence.

We find numerous examples of forgiveness sprinkled throughout the New Testament. The author of the letter to the Ephesians draws us in and sets before us a new way of dealing with one another:

³¹Put away from you all bitterness and wrath and anger and wrangling and slander, together with all malice, ³²and be kind to one another, tenderhearted, forgiving one another, as God in Christ has forgiven you. (Ephesians 4:31–32)

We witness the perfect example of the scriptural principle of forgiveness at work when Jesus was on the cross. Fighting for his life with each breath, bearing the weight of his own body on the cross, battered and bruised and bloody from being whipped and beaten, Jesus put this principle into practice when he called out, "Father, forgive them; for they do not know what they are doing." (Luke 23:34). Could we do the same? Could we forgive after suffering the same level of abuse? For some of us, it's simply too much to consider.

❖ *Sacrifice*

The principle of sacrifice dominates certain areas of the New Testament. There's no getting around the fact that Jesus repeatedly stated how he would give himself up as an offering for the kingdom of God and the sins of all who live. Jesus said in John 12:24:

> "Very truly, I tell you, unless a grain of wheat falls into the earth and dies, it remains just a single grain; but if it dies, it bears much fruit."

Jesus understood the sacrifice of his life as having a fructifying effect, producing something that goes beyond what one single person can do, becoming limitless in its extension.

When prayer and sacrifice come together, we are putting into practice the principle of the giving of ourselves so that something greater may take place. When we offer up prayers, especially those of intercession, we are sacrificing our time, our energy, and our emotional assets to ask for the needs of others. Have you ever been concerned for someone and found yourself going to God for them in prayer? Bearing the weight and strain of the situation, you open your mouth and your heart to the Lord about that person. This is a sacrifice because it's time that could be spent on something else.

As most of us know, many things vie for our attention and time. Using precious moments on problems that are not our own, we throw our energy into the plight of another. Not only is the action of prayer a sacrifice, but active praying also helps us make the necessary sacrifices we need to make. Let's face it: it's hard to find the strength to fulfill our daily obligations. It's even harder to fulfill them with a good attitude. Yet heartfelt prayer produces the wisdom, energy, and willingness to sacrifice in us. Natural energy just cannot do it. Neither can our best laid intentions.

The Holy Eucharist is known as a sacrifice of thanksgiving. The word *Eucharist* is the Greek word *Eucharistia*, which literally means "thanksgiving." In worship, we give of ourselves, offering up prayers to God. At its very essence, it taps into what the Lord's Prayer offers when it states, "Thy kingdom come, thy will be done" (Matthew 6:10), meaning, "I will sacrifice my agenda, no matter how glorious it seems to me, to your overall will and purposes."

Therefore, the sacrament recalls His sacrifice and calls us to make sacrifices of thanksgiving. It is a response to sacrifice with more sacrifice. The prayer of thanksgiving models it, demonstrating from start to finish this principle. Thus, prayer, both individual and corporate, embodies the same self-giving spirit. When we give up time, we give up something to see about someone else's needs and ask God to act on their behalf. As a newly ordained priest, I work for a rector who required us to say the Daily Office, which includes morning and evening prayer. Arriving at the chapel early in the morning daily, and most of the time half-awake, we would settle into our prie-dieu (prayer desks) and prepare ourselves for the rhythm of the routine. As part of our daily pattern, it served as a regular sacrifice that we made for the community. Real words, real prayers, to a real God, in search of real answers, fueled our time together. At the end of each day full of church duties in ministry assignments—oftentimes cutting things short to make it back on time for prayer—we would stumble back into that same dark chapel, press ourselves into those hard, wooden seats, and enter that rhythm once again. There was a sacrifice to it because we made decisions about what we would take on and what we would avoid to be back on time to pray together, as was our holy habit.

To say that sacrifice is connected to scripture, in principle, is an understatement. Moses made a sacrifice of his time and effort to shoulder the burden of leading the children of Israel out of slavery in Egypt and deliver them from the hand of Pharaoh (Exodus 3:1–22). Samuel was willing to sacrifice his time in prayer for the people of Israel, even though they had moved away from doing God's will by selecting Saul as king and, therefore, abandoning a theocracy to embrace a monarchy (1 Samuel 9). Elijah sacrificed his time and energy to be a faithful witness to live consistently for God in a time of idolatry, while Elijah encountered sacrifice when he visited the widow, who only had a small amount of oil and food as she and her son faced the threat of starvation. Yet she sacrificed herself for the benefit of the Elijah when he came to stay with her, forgoing the natural urge to keep the food for her and her son (1 Kings 17:7–24).

We encounter this principle in the New Testament as well. The founders of the early church decided that they were going to sacrifice trying to meet all the needs of the people and dedicate themselves to prayer and spirituality, which eventually moved them to ordain seven deacons to do the work of outreach among them (Acts 7). The apostle Paul, throughout his ministry, sacrificed his health, safety, and basic comforts to spread the good news of God in Christ. In Philippians 2:17, he went as far as to refer to his life as a drink offering, which was a liquid offering added to the burnt offering. Being pour upon the altar, the liquid became steam and completely evaporated through the interaction of the intense heat of the altar. For Paul, his entire life took on the same experience. Being completely spent on one thing, completely poured out, Paul had nothing left to give for any other reason. What a rich metaphor. Yet his post-Damascus experience of life embodied the spirit of this metaphor. The self-giving love that was modeled in Jesus, found its home in Paul, and expressed itself in the form of self-sacrifice for the spreading of the gospel. His actions, evangelism, thoughtful insight, and prayer life reflected the spirit of sacrifice.

In every letter he wrote to the churches, he reflected on how he was always giving thanks and praying for them. This was his pattern, which revealed a willingness to sacrifice at its core. Paul believed that both living and dying, and any suffering that took place in between, was for the sake of the gospel. He was willing to sacrifice his momentary comfort for the ongoing mission of the church.

For the most part, Paul did not see himself as giving up anything. Hosea 6:6 states: "For I desire steadfast love and not sacrifice, the knowledge of God rather than burnt offerings." We get a sense that Paul worked this out daily by knowing God and experiencing his steadfast love. It was all a loving response to God who first loved him, showcasing where Paul was at in his heart and soul.

Therefore, when we actively exercise this principle in our own lives, what we forgo may not feel like a sacrifice at all, mainly because it will come from a place of deep and abiding love. The ongoing interaction with Christ on the behalf of others, and the spiritual growth we experience as a result of such exchanges, guards us against the remorse we would feel if we were to believe we have given up too much. According to Paul, he gave up nothing. He was completely convinced that what was gained far outweighed what he lost.

The challenge for each one of us is to understand the gain in comparison to the perceived loss.

❖ *Faith*

To be committed to prayer, it is necessary to have faith in God and believe he moves in time and space, and to express concern for humanity. The Bible says in Hebrews chapter 11 verse 1, "Now faith is the assurance of things hoped for, the conviction of things not seen."

The scriptures are full of faith-filled words expressed by trusting people to a trustworthy God.

In the Bible, we see faith and hope mentioned together often, leaving us with the impression that they are quite similar and that they work together as a dynamic duo. In some ways, they are as they both have a belief in God's power to make something happen. The major difference between the two is that hope is directed toward the future and faith is concerned about the present. So one is future tense, and the other is present tense. When prayer and hope come together in the believer, it becomes a personal statement, saying, "I believe God will do something in the future." However, when prayer is combined with faith, we believe God is doing something right now, and in the urgency and importance of right now, impacts what will come.

God is working on our behalf when prayer is mixed with faith. This becomes our confidence. It's not a confidence that believes God *will* do something, but rather a confidence believing God *is* doing something about the future.

In practical terms, this means that when we converse with God, we are trust God to answer our prayers. In a business decision, it's asking for ideas. When we find ourselves having to choose between two good things, it means asking for the wisdom to know what's best. It sometimes means asking for opportunities to present themselves to you and asking for the wisdom to recognize those opportunities and capitalize on them. In relationships, it's knowing that God is working on our behalf when it comes to our human interactions. Somehow, faith and prayer work together to bring grace to difficult relationships. Somehow, faith and prayer team up to broaden the scope of our empathy when we are dealing with one another. Faith mixed with prayer is about trusting God's presence in prayer when we don't feel it and giving the benefit of the doubt to what scripture and tradition teach us. This sort of praying encompasses career, marriage, and growing families with all their challenges. Inevitably, this sort of praying addresses the issue of dying a graceful death.

Faith's role in prayer goes beyond theory and enters a new space. An example of this is what Elijah experienced when he prayed and it didn't rain for three years. Then Elijah prayed again, and the rain was restored (1 Kings 18:41–19:8 and James 5:17). This is similar to what Jesus said in Luke 17:6, "If you had faith the size of a mustard seed, you could say to this mulberry tree, 'Be uprooted and planted in the sea,' and it would obey you." It does. It also bumps against the poignancy in Jesus's words when he declared in Mark 11:24, "So I tell you, whatever you ask for in prayer, believe that you have received it, and it will be yours."

Now, this is not faith in faith. No, faith in faith is merely optimism, bereft of any real substance, lacking genuine faith. Most of the time, when placed under the microscope, faith in faith always seems to be short-lived and weak, probably because it's more of a gimmick than a spiritual exercise. You see, genuine faith in Christ is robust and resilient enough to take the bumps and bruises of everyday living. This sort of faith might cringe at the diagnosis of cancer, but it will never cower in the corner and stay there. When your spouse punches you in the gut with a request for a divorce, this sort of faith straightens your back, while you go through the process and proceedings. During stormy times, when you ask God for the strength to deal with something that is beyond your control, this sort of faith-filled prayer will give you peace in the middle of the storm. Disease comes, broken relationships happen, storm clouds emerge on the horizon of everyone's life, but faith formed and forged by a faithful relationship with Christ, not a faith in faith, will provide us with the spiritual wherewithal to stand firm. Faith-filled praying does this for us.

Faith in faith is an attempt to turn God into our personal genie as well. God refuses to be treated in such a manner. We can't pour quarters in God and get results. We can't manipulate God. What was characteristic of Jesus's faith, along with the faith of the early disciples, was their deep trust—void of any attempts to manipulate. Being a relational faith, their prayers and actions were punctuated with a palpable desire to see God glorified and connect with Him. Rather than a faith in faith that sought to serve themselves, they sought to serve Christ and others, which was dependent on a deep trust in God. The power of the Holy Spirit, not magic and manipulation, shaped the prayer lives of Jesus and the ancient saints, and this power continues to shape the prayer lives of modern Christians, especially those under immense pressure.

In the Acts of the Apostles 8:9–24, we encounter someone who believed he could manipulate God. Completely amazed after witnessing the signs and wonders of the Holy Spirit, Simon the Sorcerer developed a plan to manipulate the power of God for his benefit. At first glance, it seems like Simon started off well, as though he was genuinely converted to the faith and wanted to amend his ways. Verse 13 states:

> Even Simon himself believed. After being baptized, he stayed constantly with Philip and was amazed when he saw the signs and great miracles that took place.

Then something happened. Simon's old manipulative tendencies remained a constant point of contention. Verse 18 explains:

> 18Now when Simon saw that the Spirit was given through the laying on of the apostles' hands, he offered them money, 19saying, "Give me also this power so that anyone on whom I lay my hands may receive the Holy Spirit."

As you could guess, this request didn't go over well with the apostles, and they firmly rebuked him. You see, Simon's former life was still shaping his worldview—being the initial way he engaged the world. His old life and livelihood came from sorcery, which deploys the techniques of mind control and magic. Deception is at its core. Like an animal stalking prey, those doing such work look to pounce upon any opportunity given through fear, greed, or lust. Simon skillfully navigated this world for years and thrived from its practice. It was only interrupted by the message of the Gospel. However, soon after his encounter with the apostles, he experienced the pull of his former ways, tempting him to try to use God's power for his own advantage.

If we are not careful, we can fall into a similar trap, treating prayer and godly matters as a means to a selfish end rather than a means to a Christ-centered end. Some years ago, the Word of Faith movement grew in popularity because it communicated a message of achievement and success. Much of it had to do with prayer, but prayer in a way that focused on getting what we want from God, rather than focusing on spiritual growth and divine trust. This underlying belief has infected people's reason for tithing as well. The erroneous belief infers that when a person gives ten percent of their income, God will make good on their prayer requests. This is not true. God can never be our debtor. So prayers ranging from those for healing to those desiring financial successes were raised to God. Thus, the tithe and faith in faith made it both transactional and contractual.

To be fair, there were some genuine leaders in the movement. However, there were some scammers involved in it as well. Sadly, there are countless stories of people who participated in those ministries and who tithed and put into practice their faith in faith and saying all the right words and everything else associated with the prescribed formula for answered prayer, only to end up disillusioned and brokenhearted. For many, their belief that their loved ones would be healed was a tortured experience, leaving them with a sense of guilt, personal failure, and abandonment by God. Instead of experiencing God in a profound and comforting way during their illness, they experienced the exact opposite. God didn't let them down, but their prayers, based on faith in faith, failed them.

These people had been taught a formula: "One part this, two parts that, and, *voila*, God gives you what you want." However, prayer doesn't work like that. God, although far more concerned for us than we will ever know, cannot be maneuvered by prayer. Prayer, based on intimacy and faith in Christ, is an act of opening oneself to God, who revealed himself through the sacrificial love of Jesus, which reached its climax on the cross.

The Bible's position on faith, whether in scriptural principle or biblical narrative, has always found its greatest expression in the deep trust in God. In the biblical story of Abraham and Sarah, their development of trust in God is powerful. Abraham wasn't perfect by any means. He had to grow and develop. And through reading about Abraham's life and struggles, we get a chance to peep in on his process of maturation. The same could be said of Elijah, Elisha, Jeremiah, Ezekiel, and Job. In the gospels, we see it in the unwavering trust of Jesus, of course. In the Acts of the Apostles, we witness it through the wild adventures of the early pioneers of the faith, and we encounter it in the stories of their great dependence on God, often in the face of overwhelming odds and uncertain outcomes. The letters of the New Testament are also filled with this type of faith. Faith that is expressed through deep trust, empowers and enables us to encounter God in new ways.

1. *Emerson: The Mind on Fire*, Robert D. Richardson
2. *The Meaning of Prayer*, page 87, Harry Emerson Fosdick, TheClassics.us

seven

CORPORATE WORSHIP

The 1979 *Book of Common Prayer* has this to say about corporate worship, which is also understood as corporate prayer:

> In corporate worship, we unite ourselves with others to acknowledge the holiness of God, to hear God's Word to offer prayer, and to celebrate the sacraments.
> —The 1979 *Book of Common Prayer*

Corporate worship/prayer means praying together with others. Jesus saw corporate prayer as something very special and unique, chiefly because through it, people unite to communicate with God.

This is very different to the narrative we have about faith, which tells us it's all about the individual. How many times have we heard the words "my personal faith" or "my relationship with God," as though it does not involve anyone else? Yet if we look closely at what Jesus said, we will notice how He constantly insisted on prayer in the context of community. He and the apostles spoke of loving our neighbors as ourselves (Matthew 12:31), and how husbands and wives should get along so their prayers will not be hindered (1 Peter 3:7). Jesus exhibited community. His relationship with the twelve disciples was a true representation of living life within a self-selected tribe. He didn't go around as a prophet all by himself and operate as a solo act. Rather, he belonged to a real community, with all the misunderstandings, hiccups, aggravations, petty moments, warts, and all. In such a situation, he dealt with problems and demonstrated what it is to have a life of prayer with and among real people. To put it simply, his apostles were not props but genuine people, who were both amazing and flawed, but vitally important to his ministry and spirituality.

While among them, Jesus emphasized that the two greatest commandments were to love God and love one's neighbor, meaning they feed into one another (Matthew 22:36–40). To him, the element of neighbor cannot be divorced from prayer because fellowship to God and being a part of the community of worshippers is connected. This model extends to what is recorded in the book of Acts, with disciples going out in teams of two or more. However, there are a couple of examples when people functioned by themselves, like Philip the Evangelist, but for the most part, the apostles and disciples functioned within a community and in prayerful groups gathered for a common purpose.

❖ Stronger Together

One of the marks of the brilliance of the ministry of Jesus is how he managed to call "strong" what others in his era labeled "weak." For instance, under the tyranny of the Roman Empire, being a servant was a low and unenviable position—something to be avoided at all costs. People worked hard to avoid, and sometimes even killed, in order to keep from becoming someone's servant. In contrast, Jesus invested power in and gave dignity to what others considered weak, saying, "Whoever wants to be greatest among you must be your *servant*" (Mark 10:43). This was radical and countercultural in the day of Christ, and it remains radical and countercultural today.

Today, we are very much invested in the concept of the self-made person. Ralph Waldo Emerson's 1841 essay "Self-Reliance" is imprinted on the very soul of our nation. Over the years, we have developed the myth of the bootstrapping American, who doesn't need anyone's help. Like it or not, it has seeped into American religion, especially Christianity, and is almost impossible to overcome. Although there has been great concern and criticism around how American Christianity has become more about "self-help" than the communal, and what it has morphed into should not surprise us. To put it simply, it is basically *me-ism* taken to the next level.

In contrast, when we look directly into the very nature of the first century church and its spiritual stance, and life together, we can't help but see reliance on one another as a source of strength rather than weakness.

So let's explore what Jesus meant when He said in Matthew 18:20–22, "When two or three are gathered together in my name, I am in the midst of them." Through the intersection of God and neighbor, spiritual power is harnessed and leveraged. In essence, it creates synergy. We are all familiar with the idea of synergy. People like Stephen Covey and others have proposed the idea that one plus one doesn't exactly equal two. The powerful nature of synergy means that one plus one equals three, and sometimes equals four, perhaps even five—if the right people are involved. This means that we are infinitely more effective together, than apart. The same goes for relationships and business ventures, and it even extends to prayer and worship. Another way of putting it is the old saying, "Many hands make the work light." Having spiritual synergy basically means we come together spiritually.

Together, we are stronger, more powerful, and more active than when we are by being spiritual lone rangers. Even though this lone ranger mentality is a big part of American culture—which has crept into religion—Jesus did not intend for the Christian church to be a church of lone rangers. The health and vitality of the Christian faith is directly related to our ability to love one another and interact positively with one another in the presence of God. Thus, one of the most natural expressions of this is connected to corporate worship and corporate prayer.

The apostles also made this clear in their writings when stating in Hebrews 10:25, "Let us not give up the habit of meeting together, as some are doing." They were keenly aware of the synergy created through prayer and fellowship. They relied on one another and did not mind embracing an age-old wisdom that we somehow ignore today. This sort of reliance was their structure and it provided great support—and all of us need support. In corporate worship, we are surrounded by those who care for us and worship a God who cares for us, and we sense support in ways that are both tangible and intangible. In the liturgy of the Episcopal Church, as well as in the liturgies of most mainline denominations, there are prayers for the sick and shut in. So for those who are housebound, in the hospital or away from the parish, the prayers and support of the community provide continuity and a palpable spiritual presence.

Not only does corporate prayer provide support, but it also provides spiritual strength through formation. Through a life of prayer with others, spiritual strength increases. I remember when I was preparing to go to the seminary back in the early 1990s. I spoke to several ministers about the seminary experience and found it to be very helpful. I remember, in one conversation, I put forward the idea of working while in the seminary and going through the experience as a commuter student. As many people know, this is becoming the norm for many seminary students. So I proposed the idea and remember what the priest said to me, as if it were yesterday: "Try not to. You see, the most valuable experience of the seminary is the life we live together—worshipping together, having conversations and disagreements, and building community. This goes far beyond what you can achieve in ordinary class time and reading." He was right. Looking back, I know that through the arguments I had won and, more so, the arguments I had lost, I was made stronger in my faith in Christ. Through the humbling interactions with people holding differing theological perspectives, my beliefs were tested, strengthened, and given space to develop. In the first year of the seminary, I realized that I wasn't as great a Christian as I'd thought I was, and my understanding of the grace of God became more robust. The seminary was just the beginning of a fortifying process that has lasted throughout my entire ministry. I've been made stronger by the people I've had contact with, prayed with, and worshipped with. This is true for you as well. No one is an island.

Lastly, corporate worship provides perspective. The burial liturgy for the Episcopal Church includes scriptures from the book of Revelation. In chapter 7, the apostle John paints a picture of an entire community of people standing before the Lamb who was on the throne, worshiping him and giving him glory. This was a large group of people—a collective. Repeatedly, we see references to the community before Christ. Community is at God's heart; it is part of God's desire. However, this doesn't mean individual faith is not important—it is. It's very important. Private devotion, ongoing scripture reading, a disciplined and passionate prayer life, the personal challenge to embrace the commands of the gospel, all of these are markers of individual faith. However, it doesn't stop there. When our individual strengths come together with the strength of the community, real transformation takes place, and amazing prayer results happen. It's almost as if through community, prayer develops into an action plan. The relationships of the community provide a prospective on life that can't be experienced independently.

❖ *Eucharist as Consummate Model of Corporate Prayer*

I had an aha moment when I learned in my liturgical class that a priest can never celebrate the Eucharist (communion) all by him- or herself. It spoke volumes to how necessary it is to have my brother or sister present in the act of worship. However, there were practical reasons for it. In the medieval period of the church, the practice of private Eucharist/mass was abused. People would pay local priests to say a private mass as memorial for their deceased love ones. The practice, grounded in the belief of masses celebrated for the dead would secure heaven for them, thrived during this period. Private masses for the dead grew in popularity, resulting in the proliferation of altars and priest whose only work was to do private masses. The Church of England, after separating from the Catholic Church, chose to jettison the practice altogether. This made a statement as the two chief sacraments of the church—baptism and Eucharist—were required to be public and communal acts of prayer and worship.

The role of the sacraments in joining us together reminds me of the Zulu word *ubuntu*. It literally means "I am because of you." Its meaning challenges our ideals on human interaction. It underscores the vital importance of community. Nelson Mandela believed that the theory and practice of ubuntu needed to be part of the future of South Africa. Upon becoming president, he sought to organize the government along this principle. Mandela knew "I am because of you" had to be the calling card of living a life together.

In the life of the church, what would it be like if we experienced ubuntu among ourselves? What would happen if we embraced the corporate nature of the sacraments? What insights would we gain and what goals would we achieve if we said to each other within the walls of the church, "I am who I am because of you"? What would happen if we touched our local communities in such a way that they could say to us, "We are who we are because of you, the local church." Wouldn't it be amazing? What would happen if we lived God's purpose for our local church communities? If we could do so, transformation would take place. This is highlighted in the words of Jesus when he said in John 14:12(NIV), "And *they* [meaning *us*] will do even greater things."

eight

THE HOLY SPIRIT'S
ROLE IN PRAYER

U sing his outstretched arms to steady himself against the wooden lectern, sleeves rolled up, he peered over his glasses and scanned the classroom. Then, slowly and softly, he spoke to us saying, "I want to conduct an experiment with you today. I want you to close your eyes and listen to what I have to say. If you ever had an experience you couldn't explain, but you knew it was God, with your eyes still closed, raise your hands."

I thought, *Okay, I can do this, since no one will see. I certainly don't want to be the strange one in the class.* It was true, the class included a former dean of a medical school, a retired owner of a chemical company, and a historical preservationist, just to name a few. No one wanted to stand out for experiencing something strange. But with all eyes closed and therefore free of judgmental gazes, I raised my hand.

"Okay," he said, "those of you who raised your hands can put them down. Now, open your eyes!" he instructed. Then he remarked, "Because your eyes were closed, you couldn't see it, but almost every hand in the class went up in response to my question." Even though this was a New Testament class at a theological seminary, we were surprised. He went on to talk about the common experiences people have but rarely speak of. These run-ins with the Holy Spirit, these inexplicable occasions that add to the mystery of God, serve to remind us of how something far beyond our ability to comprehend is working behind the scenes.

When we contemplate prayer, we must consider the Holy Spirit's role in it. The Holy Spirit gives us the desire to pray and in fact, He is the Spirit of prayer.

Romans 8:26 says, "Likewise the Spirit helps us in our weakness; for we do not know how to pray as we ought, but that very Spirit intercedes with sighs too deep for words."

But what does that mean for us, really? It means our thoughts naturally turn to the subject of the Holy Spirit. In scripture, we have awe-inspiring descriptions of the work of the Holy Spirit, which capture our imaginations and stir excitement in us regarding the possibilities of God's power. So what's so special about the Holy Spirit, and what is His role in prayer?

❖ The Holy Spirit Is a Person

Primarily and theologically, the Holy Spirit is a person—the third person of the Godhead, the Trinity. The three creeds of Christianity address this. Where the Nicene and Apostles Creeds touch on it slightly, the Athanasian Creed goes to great lengths in its treatment of the Holy Spirit, since the creed's original intent was to articulate the nature and co-equality of the Holy Trinity. The Holy Spirit should never be referred to as "it," and is therefore purposely addressed as a person. He is an active personality in the world-wide church and in the day-to-day lives of every individual believer.

Let's put it this way. God deals with you and me daily and speaks to us through the actions and influences of the Holy Spirit. He might nudge us to speak with someone about something God has placed in our hearts. Perhaps, he might inspire us to visit someone who is in the hospital or to take care of someone in need. Sometimes, it takes the shape of speaking the truth to power when our neighbors suffer abuse. At times, when we experience the inexplicable, as my New Testament professor said years ago, we are participating in a dance with the Holy Spirit. In every dance couple, there is a lead partner, and the Holy Spirit is our lead partner. When you truly feel led to do something—something that is empowering and life-giving, or something that restores or upholds human dignity—the

Holy Spirit is involved. He is a personality that interacts with us. This personality extends to prayer. The long-standing belief of the universal church, from its inception to present day, is the Spirit prays through us, and according to Acts 8:26, "We do not know what we ought to pray for, but the Spirit intercedes."

❖ The Holy Spirit's Pastoral Presence

The Bible has some pastoral insights about the Holy Spirit as well. In John 14:26, Jesus called the Holy Spirit "the Comforter." Ancient and modern saints alike have written about the comfort of the Holy Spirit. While amid the storms of life, these saints have often described a feeling of comfort and confidence in God that no person or material item could give them. So, when we are going through times when there is a lot of discontent and disillusionment, pressure and anxiety, knowing that the Holy Spirit is a comforter, can do wonders for your blood pressure.

There are, as well, pastoral implications in John 16:13, which refers to the Holy Spirit as the Spirit of Truth:

> "When the Spirit of truth comes, he will guide you into all the truth...."

This means He leads with our best intentions in mind, guiding us to make wise decisions and pursue the right direction. As we journey with God, the truth becomes more and more apparent over time.

I once heard an old story about truth. It's the story of the race between the turtle and the greyhound. The turtle (known as *The Truth*) and the greyhound (known as *The Lie*) challenged each other to a race. The starting pistol was fired and off they went. As anyone can assume, the greyhound (*The Lie*) instantly took the lead and finished the race in about thirty minutes. The turtle (*The Truth*) on the other hand, took its sweet time—as turtles normally do—and finished two months later. It took the turtle (*The Truth*) so long to finish that people had almost forgotten there was a race in the first place.

When asked, "What took you so long?" the turtle (*The Truth*) said, "When I arrive, you know things are right, that's why." And this is true.

There are lies we can believe about life, which promote selfishness and material gain as central to life. But the truth will emerge. This applies to the lies we believe about one another as well. Gossip, rumors, and innuendos spring forth rather quickly, taking hold of people's imaginations, at least for a while. They always damage things further. The truth nonetheless will emerge eventually. The truth of God's love for humanity, the truth of our need of relationship with God and one another, the truth of the inability of material things to give peace, all of these are truths poised to present themselves when we are opened to hearing from the Holy Spirit.

Retired professor of molecular biology Dr. Cliff Campbell once shared his grandmother's wisdom on truth with me. She said, "If it doesn't come out in the wash, it will definitely come out in the rinse." When the truth arrives, as it always does, it exposes the lie. When the truth arrives, it brings health where disease once reigned. When the truth arrives, it sheds light where darkness once prevailed. When truth is sought and discovered, things are made right. The Holy Spirit, according to Jesus, deals in truth and leads us to truth.

So John 16:13 opens us up to the pastoral presence of the Holy Spirit by His relationship with truth. On one level, it means the discovery of the truth of who and what Jesus is. Therefore, the Holy Spirit's role in guiding us into truth means understanding we are persons with spiritual concerns and ultimately, our spiritual interests will lead us to Christ. On another level, there is a broader sense of this truth, one that reveals to us deeper truths about God, ourselves, or our ability to be change agents. It even means, when considering all of life's challenges, how we come in contact with the truth of the endless possibilities that might be attached to the problem and how they may ultimately serve as occasions to underscore the greatness of God.

✧ *The Holy Spirit Lives in You*

Now, get this, because it's huge: the Holy Spirit lives inside of you. This means that by His presence, He directly impacts our identities. Years ago, this quote found its way into an Upper Room publication: "Unless there is within us that which is above us, we shall soon yield to that which is about us." Yet because of God, we are more than what surrounds us. The Bible clearly states in 1 Corinthians 6:19 how each individual Christian is the temple of the Holy Spirit:

> Or do you not know that your body is a temple of the Holy Spirit within you, which you have from God, and that you are not your own?

Do you see yourself as God's holy temple? You should, because the Holy Spirit dwells in us in the new birth, which is outwardly marked by baptism. In 1 Corinthians 3:16, we are also collectively called the temple of the Holy Spirit. It states: "Don't you know that you yourselves [the Church] are God's temple and that God's Spirit dwells in your midst?" The apostle Paul calls us God's holy temple. All of this is designed for God to live in us and to work through us to touch others. Through the Holy Spirit's presence, we are ever reminded of who we are and to whom we belong.

❖ *The Spirit of Ministry*

But wait! There's more. God's sovereign work is on display when the Holy Spirit is poured out on us and we are filled with the Holy Spirit to do ministry. One of the ways in which we know the Holy Spirit is assisting our ministry is because it glorifies God the Father and Jesus Christ through His entire effort. Jesus even said that the Holy Spirit does not seek to glorify himself but rather seeks to glorify the Son (John 16:15). So whatever we do, He will give glory to God, even when we don't use words. People will experience the presence of God in your actions, in the loving way you serve meals to the homeless, in the respect you give to those others overlook and dismiss. Through the Spirit, we become larger than the obstacles we face, and He helps us serve others out of the generous resource of God's great love.

We touched on the Holy Spirit's ministry in theory. However, what does it look like on the ground? How does it take shape in practical ways? Well, we see it in a mother that I knew in Pennsylvania who had a son who suffered from juvenile diabetes. His illness, although not as bad as many others, is still one that impacted his activities and life in general. The mother, who was a tremendous singer, produced a music cd and used the proceeds from sales to help fund the battle against the disease. Here, the Holy Spirit used her talent and her son's issue to bring others to God's glory. Through ample prayer, under the influence of the Holy Spirit, our issues and challenges become opportunities for ministry. In the case of the woman in Pennsylvania, the Holy Spirit took her on a journey full of unfolding truths about her son's diabetes. Through the Spirit's role in ministry, He inspired her, and He will inspire us to intercede in specific needs. Consider this: the Holy Spirit is looking to do something through us when we depend on Him in prayer.

nine

THE IMPACT OF PRAYER ON COMMUNITIES

Prayer does not mean simply to pour out one's heart. It means rather to find the way to God and to speak with Him, whether the heart is full or empty.

—Dietrich Bonhoeffer, twentieth-century martyr and theologian

When churches and faith-based organizations apply themselves to grow in prayer, especially intercessory prayer, it creates a transformative concern within the life of the community, one so powerful that it can change the prevailing story and insert a whole new narrative. It pulls groups and individuals focusing on their own concerns and it pushes them into situations and concerns of others. This has always been part of the role of prayer. In so many ways, the Holy Spirit pulls us out of our own selfish natures and moves us to embrace what is worthwhile in others—to invest in a dream that is not our own. Prayer compels us to look toward our neighbor, who is not like us but who we are called to love, nonetheless. When the church engages in the constant practice of prayer, especially intercessory prayer, it moves beyond its normal constraints, beyond the thoughts and concerns of budgets and organizational growth, and finds itself involved in the deep concerns of its disaffected neighbors.

When this happens, the church gets involved in the struggles, burdens, and complexities of the day-to-day lives of its neighbors. It's a known fact that when we pray, we think more broadly and deeply and our empathy expands. This sort of prayer allows us to ask, "How can I be most helpful to my neighbor?"

In the parish where I serve, our prayers, worship, and the life we live together bring about a synergy that pushes us to go beyond what typically concerned us. However, anxieties about our budget did not go away. We still struggle with this challenge that every local church struggles with: to find creative ways in which to grow our congregation. Year after year, we experience the pressures of attrition. There are always those who leave due to having to move away, or who needed to move on in their faith journey by joining another congregation or those who have gone to be with the Lord in death. So our challenges are not unique, but we experience them through the grace and comfort of the Holy Spirit, which places us in conversation with the possibilities, and helps us see that there's so much more to be done.

What my parish and other spiritual communities are experiencing is something known as disruptive empathy. The French philosopher Rene Girard defined it as "the moment when our empathy with the other becomes so genuine, so real, that it changes our live and we are willing to step out our daily routine and reach out help that person. When that happens, we are longer able to act as though the injustice around us has nothing to do with us, and are more will to stand with the other person and share their fate." By means of the Incarnation, Jesus came into our world as the "other," probably more than anyone in history because he entered human space from the heavenly point of origination. He experienced disruptive empathy more clearly because He was an outsider in every way, even in his own community and family. We, however, struggle to enter that space on a different level because we are divided by self-imposed differences of race and class, and the very real but exaggerated differences of gender.

As described by Professor Victoria Barnett, PhD, disruptive empathy means being a neighbor on a whole new level and makes our old understanding of what it is to be a neighbor seem inadequate. It raises the stakes and requires that we dive more deeply into the messy situations of others, taking our interconnectedness to the next level or better yet, the level God always intended for human interaction. It drives home the idea, as my priest friend Martha Francis once put it, that "we are called, not just as *partners*, but as *accomplices*." This means that no matter what takes place, we have skin in the game.

In her lecture "From Harlem to Berlin" at Beeson Divinity School, Professor Barnett stated how this kind of empathy appeared in the life of the German martyr, Dietrich Bonhoeffer. In 1930, with the help of international friends, he left Germany and planted himself in the United States, becoming part of the community of the Union Theological Seminary in New York City. While at Union, Bonhoeffer befriended Franklin Fisher, an African-American seminarian from Birmingham, Alabama, who introduced him to the rich worship culture of African-Americans in New York City's Abyssinian Baptist Church. His empathy, Barnett suggests, budded as he experienced the spiritual vibrancy of the black community and observed how their faith sustained their spiritual composure and human dignity in the face of relentless racial discrimination and violence. Bonhoeffer found himself outraged by the pre-civil rights plight of African-Americans and started to draw parallels with the anti-Semitism that was occurring in Germany.

Bonhoeffer's experiences were seeded in something new and heartfelt when he came to the side of the Jews who were suffering in Nazi Germany. Bonhoeffer was keenly aware of how deeply imbedded anti-Semitism was within the culture and became more painfully aware of how he and even the best intentioned around him, had comprised in one way or another. Not always possessing the courage and commitment he is presently known for, Dr. Barnett suggests that Bonhoeffer grew into his resolve gradually, one step at a time, one day at a time, one experience at a time, and eventually coming to understand that all human life is intertwined. Bonhoeffer developed a moral stance similar to the one advanced years later by the Dr. Martin Luther King Jr. in his letter from a Birmingham jail, which declared one person falling victim to injustice was direct violation of the dignity of all of humanity. Due to our interconnectedness the plight of one is tied to the plight of all. It's inescapable. For Bonhoeffer, and for King after him, the act of prayer provided them with the sort of empathy that caused them to act. In this, Bonhoeffer was not naïve or idealistic. Bearing witness to his ground in reality, Bonhoeffer's book, *Life Together,* dealt with the messiness of community and explained how disillusionment with ourselves is the necessary ingredient for a Christian life and how it nourishes the soul and uses our individual and communal brokenness to powerfully and effectively touch the world around us. In this sense, he saw the work of prayer not as the initiative of perfect people but the humble and faithful response to an even more faithful God who humbled himself to the point of taking on human flesh.

> Since meditation on the Scriptures, prayer, and intercession are a service we owe and because the grace of God is found in this service, we should train ourselves to set apart a regular hour for it, as we do for every other service we perform. This is not "legalism"; it is orderliness and fidelity. (87)

The compound interest of Bonhoeffer's risky engagement in human affairs and his radically simplified understanding of Christian witness allowed him to evolve as a minister, and eventually compelled him to do something about his home country. Similarly, King did the same on behalf of a community of people who were of his own racial background. However, his mission evolved to include all poor people everywhere. King's subsequent martyrdom was directly connected to the eventual turn in his focus, one in which disruptive empathy obligated him to pronounce a poor people's campaign and then denounce the Vietnam War.

Over time, and through different experiences, both Bonhoeffer and King showed such a deep concern for the welfare of others that their lives were completely disrupted and they were compelled to go beyond their comfort zones. Active and authentic prayer anchored these two titans in their faith and developed their respective relationship with God, and increased their capacity for empathy.

This is how prayer worked in the lives of two legendary Christian martyrs and how it works in the lives of ordinary believers. Prayer drives us beyond our comfort zones, directing us to look at the stark realities around us and forces us to make decisions. A person who is a true intercessor, someone who places at the feet of God the cares and concerns of other people, cannot walk away from the experiences of prayer without undergoing change, especially when praying for communities that have been beaten down by economic hardship, environmental racism, or a myriad of other issues. Voicing our fears and frustrations to God amid incidents of school shootings, widespread institutional erosion, or uttering penitential, vulnerable words in a world where admitting fault is seen as a weakness or at best, unnecessary, is disruptive. Living by faith, not in an attempt to manipulate God into doing what we want but rather to trust God more deeply, is disruptive. After surveying all the needs that exist in the world, it is disruptive to ask God, "What can I do to help? What role must I play? What must I do to make things better?"

Miles J. Unger, in describing the ceiling of the Sistine Chapel, remarked that it "is a raging tempest in which God is no longer a comforting presence but a surging, disruptive power" (*Michelangelo: A Life in Six Masterpieces*, Miles J. Unger, 165). We are God's work of art, and we are still in process. Physically, divine disruption is powerfully depicted in the masterpiece on the chapel's ceiling and spiritually, it should be an ongoing theme painted on the canvases—the individual lives—of every single believer.

Through prayer, Christian communities of the past experienced great disruption. In England, from 1790 to 1830, a Christian group called the Clapham Sect experienced its unsettling force. William Wilberforce and other members of the Clapham Sect were aware of the bitter realities of trafficking African bodies in slavery and the multi-generational carnage of that awful institution. By working through the church, parliament, and the common secular avenues, the Clapham Sect changed the country.

Across the pond in North America, the Lord disrupted the normalcy of the Quakers' peaceful lives as they grew tired of witnessing the practice of slavery, which they deemed inhumane and antithetical to the gospel. At one time, benefiting from the despicable institution, this prayer-centered community, which vigorously communicated with God through active listening, trusting and speaking, found themselves at odds with slavery. Unlike their brethren in other Christian denominations scattered throughout the southern region of the United States, they could not reconcile their theology and way of life. The disconnect that existed between belief and practice created unbearable tensions among them, and they found themselves completely turning from it. As early as 1688, the Society of Friends condemned the vile practice of chattel slavery, drawing a line of demarcation between them and their slave-holding neighbors. Much like what Bonhoeffer and King would do later in history, the Quakers' convictions, supported by prayer, moved them far beyond simply condemning it and led them to be vital players in the abolition movement and becoming collaborators in the Underground Railroad. One very notable example was the role of Anna and Ellen Richardson, two Quakers who raised money to purchase Frederick Douglass's freedom while he resided in Britain and was considered a fugitive slave under United States law.

Whether it is slavery, fascism, anti-Semitism, civil rights, or any current issues that have emerged and have caused great concern, our communication with God, which is the pouring out of our very selves to him, connects us to the situations of others.

So what are you praying about that disrupts you? What makes you reevaluate your level of access and privilege? Are you reconsidering your life in connection to the lives of others—lives that are just as valuable as yours in the eyes of God?

When God disrupts our lives, putting to death the old, worthless ideas that ruled our behavior and influenced our choices, something new and healthy sprouts in their place. What was useless and unproductive becomes like the chaff that is thrown out and burned up with an unquenchable fire, as Matthew 3:12 puts it. In such a way, our conversations with God change our actions, attitudes, and perspective. In this way, we enter the level of empathy and engagement in which Jesus operated.

ten

THANKSGIVING

> What if we woke up today only to receive what we thanked
> God for yesterday?
> —A billboard on Highway 45 between Dallas
> and Houston that caught the attention of Dr. Joe
> Bedford, parishioner of Saint James', Houston

It was the fall of 1999. The leaves of the trees were changing colors—
crimson, yellow, and orange. The beauty of fall in Massachusetts was
all around me. I took a jaunt to Cambridge to go to the Society of Saint
John the Evangelist for a retreat. As part of my agreement with the church
I was with, I was required to take two retreats a year—a measure set in
place to make sure one's spiritual life remained active and never became an
afterthought. I arrived at the monastery with a bag full of books, expecting
to read everything I hadn't had the time to read while I was involved in a
full pastoral schedule. All pastors make time for reading—it's a must—but
rarely do we have the opportunity to read as much as we feel we ought. So,
entering my small room, I emptied my bag and begin to stack my books
on the desk nestled against the wall, right beneath the window. *I am going
to get a lot of reading done*, I thought. I hurried to put my things away so
I could be prepared to do what was next on the agenda: a meeting with
my spiritual director.

The spiritual director's office was small and dark. He greeted me and invited me to sit down in one of the two chairs that were facing each other. He wore a white habit, which is the regular attire of the brothers of the order. After prayer and a somewhat uncomfortable moment of silence, he asked me, "What do you plan to do during this spiritual retreat?"

I answered, "Oh, well, pray, of course." Then, letting out a sigh, I continued, "And there's a lot of reading I want to do. I mean, I brought a lot of books to read, and I really can't wait to get into them." Then, I went on a dump about the different books I had brought and their various subjects. As I spoke, he listened stoically. Once I ran out of nervous words, we sat in a moment of silence once again, equal in duration to the first but greater in discomfort. We sat there, looking at one another as though we were in a standoff in an old Western movie. However, he and I were not a sheriff and villain preparing for a shootout and trying to see who was quicker on the draw. Instead, we were two fellow travelers on the same road that had been trekked by millions over many years. Their journey, as well as mine and the man in the white habit sitting before me, ultimately leads to a savior who lived and died and rose again some two thousand years ago. Then, out of the silence he spoke, "Don't worry about the books. That's *doing*. Instead, I want you to remain present here and just *be*. I want you to start off by going down to the River Charles, and just walk beside it and think about your life and your relationship with God and offer thanks. Simply, offer thanks!"

Gratitude is the disposition of the heart; it is a way of being in the world that gives credit where credit is due. Sometimes we forget, but there will always be an abundance of things for which to be thankful. We can be thankful for health, opportunities, family, the freedoms we have, education, and even lessons learned in the school of hard knocks—you name it. There are myriad reasons for which to give thanks.

Yet, for all the reasons to give thanks to God, so few actually do. Rather than being grateful, many fall victim to ingratitude, choosing to concentrate on what hasn't been done rather than what has been done for them, and fixating on what they don't have rather than appreciating what they do have. It's a poor way to live. It's even a poorer way to exist before a giving God.

A lot of factors go into people's ingratitude. Most of us are consumed with making comparisons and evaluating our own lives along the side of the lives of others, trying to see if we have the same advantages they have—real or perceived. One of the insidious problems inherent to social media is the tendency for people to present their best lives by displaying photos of extravagant vacations and amazing birthday parties, and painting the picture of an enviable life. In the end, it's not reality. First, it's not the purpose of social media, or at least it shouldn't be. The goal of social media was to connect people, not elicit envy. Correct? When we look at such things, we become dissatisfied with our lot in life, ultimately forming a case to protest what we have and do not have. This is not right. We need to be able to say, "God, I praise you and I thank you for all that I have each and every day."

The scriptures repeatedly show us examples of people in difficult situations, who had the presence of mind to give God the glory, praise, and thanks he deserves. Psalm 34 is remarkable in this sense, when it states, "I will bless the Lord at all times; his praise shall continually be in my mouth." David came to these words under some tough circumstances. He was being tracked down by King Saul, who had a singular interest in killing him. He was on the run and in a desperate condition. Yet, when he looked through the lens of God's love and faithfulness, he couldn't help but be thankful and give God praise.

This is evident in the New Testament as well, for 1 Thessalonians 5:18 declares, "Give thanks in all circumstances; for this is the will of God in Christ Jesus for you." No matter what situation we find ourselves, we give thanks.

Thanksgiving is a required response to God. Most of the time it is an immediate reaction to God's goodness and obvious help in a tough time—a met need or deliverance from a dangerous situation. Sometimes, however, it's a deliberate act of the will in less than desirable situations, when we would like to curse our circumstances. During hard times, it's helpful to remember both the commandment to give thanks and the numerous reasons we were able to give thanks in the past. No matter how it comes about, it must take place. In this, ancient saints knew something many of us don't: praying with gratitude is healing, appropriate, and the most honest response we can give to God.

Every season of life has an opportunity for thanksgiving built into it. After we have worshipped and adored God just because He is good, and after we have prayed for the needs of others, as well as our own needs in petition, we need to give thanks. The time for giving thanks can be an opportunity to sit in silence, wherein we can allow the memories of our blessings and goodness wash over us and prompt us to recall all that God has done and is presently doing in our lives. You see, by taking a second to contemplate what God has given to us, we enter a space of gratitude. It's a humbling experience because it reminds us that everything good comes from Him.

This also means we should look at our problems through the lens of gratitude. Over the years as a pastor, one of the most puzzling things I have experienced is people who went through horrible accidents, faced terrible illnesses, or experience a tremendous loss, only to have them walk away from those times, saying, "Yet, I thank God." Theologically, I understand it, but I am always surprised to hear it because some situations seem so unimaginably painful. Yet, it is important to note that they were not thanking God for the disease, the accident, or the frustrating set of circumstances but rather, they were thanking God for his loving kindness and presence during those times. This both challenged and strengthened my faith as it forced me to reconsider the depth of my belief in the goodness of God. If we're honest, all of us go through this, and I think this is appropriate for the simple fact that it provides an opportunity for us to grow in our gratitude and our relationship with God. So thank God *not for* your problems *but through* your problems.

Give thanks during a crisis, really? Yes, exactly. Giving thanks to God during a time of crisis means we can acknowledge the role hardship and necessity play in bringing about opportunities. The crisis might be an opportunity to grow by asking new questions—questions that may take our understanding and awareness to new levels.

For example, in North American Christianity, many of the mainline denominations are experiencing a loss of membership. This is a crisis. However, we can decide whether to engage this crisis with the spirit of gratitude or to dwell on our lack of resources and dwindling numbers. Creatively, we can give thanks to God for this opportunity to ask bold, new questions. What would happen if we collectively said, "God, we thank you for this opportunity to see how we can serve in creative, new ways." Questions formed out of the spirit of gratitude, ultimately must be answered. When gratitude is coupled with such prayers, answered prayer is the ultimate result.

This is true for your personal circumstances as well. Consider what would happen if we remained grateful to God during times of difficulty. For example, "God, the divorce I'm going through is so painful right now, but I thank you for the opportunity that I had in this marriage, and I pray for the wisdom to learn from the mistakes we made. I ask you to give me the knowledge to know how I might grow from this."

The argument for gratitude builds its own case, even outside of the realm of religion. Studies have shown that there are direct health and social benefits that can be derived from gratitude and from giving thanks. For anyone, religious or not, the benefits speak for themselves. According to a 2015 article in *Psychology Today* magazine, gratitude, without question, produces the following benefits:

- Opens the door to more relationships
- Improves physical health
- Improves psychological help
- Enhances empathy and reduces aggression
- Provides better sleep
- Improves self-esteem
- Increases mental strength

This proves we have an innate need to show gratitude. To do so is an act of honoring something that is imprinted in our DNA. And when we don't do it, we suffer for it, and all the pain is self-inflicted. So, if we are truly designed to give thanks and show gratitude, we should. This goes for giving thanks to the people around us and primarily, to God.

When considering gratitude and giving thanks, the words of Melody Beattie come to mind: "Gratitude unlocks the fullness of life. It turns what we have into enough, and more. It turns denial into acceptance, chaos to order, confusion to clarity. It can turn a meal into a feast, a house into a home, a stranger into a friend." As a survivor of kidnapping and sexual abuse, it is easy to assume that gratitude was the furthest thing from Beattie's mind. She could have chosen to be locked in the spiral of ingratitude, believing life handed her nothing more than a raw deal, and no one would have held it against her. Yet this author of the best-selling novel *Codependent No More* has become a spokesperson for giving thanks.

So look at your life. Consider your own level of gratitude. Like a mechanic will use a dipstick to check the oil level and overall condition of an automobile, check the attitude of your thoughts and determine how much gratitude is there because it is one of the clues to the condition of your soul.

To sum it all up, the words of Vienna Cobb Anderson give us a small sample the things for which we can express gratitude to God:

God of all blessings, source of all life, giver of all grace:
We thank you for the gift of life:
for the breath that sustains life, for the food
of this earth that nurtures life,
for the love of family and friends without which there would be no life.
We thank you for the mystery of creation:
for the beauty that the eye can see, for the joy
that the ear may hear, for the unknown
that we cannot behold filling the universe with wonder,
for the expanse of space that draws us beyond
the definitions of our selves.
We thank you for setting us in communities:
for families who nurture our becoming, for friends who love us
by choice, for companions at work, who share our burdens and
daily tasks, for strangers who welcome us into their midst,
for people from other lands who call us to
grow in understanding, for children
who lighten our moments with delight, for the unborn,
who offer us hope for the future.
We thank you for this day:
for life and one more day to love, for opportunity and one
more day to work for justice and peace, for neighbors and
one more person to love and by whom be loved,
for your grace and one more experience of your presence,
for your promise:

to be with us, to be our God, and to give salvation.
For these, and all blessings,
we give you thanks, eternal, loving God,
through Jesus Christ we pray. Amen.

conclusion

As we bring this book to a close, let's consider the following: Moses received the Ten Commandments, Saint John had a vision that became what we know as the book of Revelation, and Jesus's inner circle - Peter James and John - witnessed his transfiguration. What do all of these profound experiences have in common? They are all accounts of what happened to people while praying. Whether clutching the rocks of Mt. Sinai or marking time on the Island of Patmos or surrounded by a core group of friends in a secluded place, these were accounts of God breaking into the lives of his faithful people, creating defining moments for them.

Our journey through prayer, in its various forms, not only explored how important they are but also served as an appeal to move forward and live as a continuance of the experiences of Moses, Jesus, and John. Their holy encounters with God came through the portal of prayer, and we are called to imitate them in the practice that created the experiences they had.

Their frank conversations with God gave them strength to deal with and pronounce victory over the system of the world that, to use the words of Bishop N. T. Wright, "was still rumbling along[11]." In the face of this system Moses gave praise to God rather than Pharaoh. In the cases of Jesus and John, the system paid fealty to Caesar. Boldly, they pronounced a new way governed by a radically different leader and infused by a different set of values and priorities. In each case, God was penetrating the old system and leaving traces of the new. We, too, live amid a world system that keeps moving forward as rapidly as ever. Yet, while it does, we are part of a kingdom system bent on overtaking it and setting things right. For every bit of sorrow and despair the old system dishes out, the kingdom

---

[11]   Interview with Bishop N. T. Wright, 200 Church Churches podcast, Episode 200.

system bestows - to a greater degree - hope, love, and genuine connection, which was modeled in the life and ministry of Jesus the Messiah. Our conversations with God are the seeds for this. Therefore, by default, our prayers are dangerous, subversive, and transformational.

Imbedded in all of us is a weighty sense that every prayer to God takes us one step closer to finding home. We are a homeward-bound people. We are encouraged to abide in this confidence and to crave the place where deep calls to deep. As Eugene Peterson, pastor, mentor, and author of The Way, once put it, "We become what we are called to be by praying."[12] So continue to seek God, secretly and often, because there is value in every step of this prayerful journey.

---

[12] Eugene Peterson, Under the Unpredictable Plant (Grand Rapids, Michigan: Wm. B Eerdmans Publishing, 1992), p 74.